Horse List
Book 3

HORSES. RIDING. LIFE.

KATHY FARROKHZAD

Photographs by Natalie Banaszak

Illustration by Jeff Thompson

A Collection of Articles From

Horse Listening: The Blog

Published by:

Full Circle Equestrian
P.O. Box 216
Ballinafad, ON, Canada N0B 1H0

www.horselistening.com

DEDICATION

To Eva, Kaleigh, Carol, Kourosh and Lynne

A Recipe For Living

You need:

– one warm, gloriously bug-free fall evening

– one soft, almost soothing "fits-like-a-glove" saddle

– one enthusiastic, steady, energetic, perky-eared red-head mare swishing rhythmically through a sweet-smelling smorgasbord of dried, crispy leaves

– one clear and wide path lined with tall trees, glowing brilliantly with hues of yellow, red, orange and green broken by a background of deep blue evening sky

– one almost indistinguishable white-tailed deer – noticed only thanks to chestnut mare's extra-sensory perception – flitting through the trees with nary a sound (how is that possible with all dried foliage on the ground)

– one busy black-bodied squirrel darting zig-zag patterns underfoot in preparation for undoubtedly colder days ahead (shattering the stillness in grizzly-like fashion)

– several mounds of sweet, luscious grass beckoning the red-head mare for a leisurely pause to quietly munch here and there

– an almost full moon gladly preparing to assume the sun's duty by reflecting light on the earth

– one human (body, mind, heart and soul) ready to appreciate it all.

Just mix and enjoy!

Contents

SAFETY FIRST

In all of this book's chapters, as in all riding, concern for the horse's well-being, health and longevity is at the forefront of our efforts. It is also the method behind the madness of all the suggestions contained in this book.

As with all physical endeavors, horseback riding requires a certain level of fitness, balance and coordination. The unpredictable nature of the horse always adds an element of uncertainty and danger that we needs to be aware of.

Please use any and all of the suggestions in this book at your discretion. Common sense always prevails! Feel free to change anything to meet the needs of you and your horse. Finally, be sure to "listen," because the horse will always let you know if you are on the right track.

INTRODUCTION

It's the horses that bring out the best in us. No matter how you slice it and dice it, living life around horses makes us reach deep down into the very core of our existence and find all that is good and giving. We don't have to compete in the show ring to reach our goals. Just interacting with horses transports us to another place of being.

This is the third book from the *Horse Listening Collection*. Based on the popular blog, these books are compilation of articles collated into themes. Maybe you have already journeyed along with me through the first two books.

Horse Listening – The Book: Stepping Forward To Effective Riding was all about the rider and how we can improve our riding skills for the sake of the horse. *Horse Listening – Book 2: Forward and Round To Training Success* focused more on the basic concepts that are required to make us better trainers for our horses.

In this book - *Horse Listening – Book 3: Horses. Riding. Life.* – we take a step back and become more introspective. The chapters present opportunities for reflection and are focused on the deep personal development that transpires when you live life in the presence of horses.

The book is divided into three sections: Horses, Riding and Life – which is in fact the tag line of the website. These three essential components describe the full experience that is horse riding.

Section 1: Horses.

Horses are different from domesticated animals like dogs and cats – they are larger than us, physically more powerful and offer us an experience unlike any other pet can do. The simple act of riding brings about entirely new skills and attitudes that must be developed in order to keep ourselves and our horses safe from harm.

As prey animals, horses engage with their environment differently than we do. So in order to be effective communicators, we must learn to focus on our body language and nonverbal intentions. We have to reach deep within ourselves to become authentic beings.

Whether working with horses from the ground or in the saddle, we become ever so sensitive to how much we need to learn even while we want to be the horse trainers. Self-reflection and self-discovery becomes a welcome side-benefit of all our horse related endeavors.

Section 2: Riding.

It's an entirely different learning process in the saddle. First off, we have to learn about skills and body parts we were never aware of. While it is true that some people are naturals when they first sit in the saddle, *all* of us have to go through fairly similar skill acquisition in the first few years. The reason is that once you've put yourself on top of a horse' s back, you're bound by the same laws of gravity as everyone else.

While you can develop a fairly deep connection with horses from the ground, the language that must develop from the back is something else. You can't possibly know what it feels like until you do it for yourself. The depth of communication you can develop with a horse from the saddle is immeasurable and can be intense at times.

This is because for a conversation to occur, there must be two at the table. And one of them is a flight animal ten times your weight, whose legs are the only ones to touch the ground! This is when you learn so much; first, about being empathic towards another being, and second, about who you really are.

Riding can develop so many "soft" skills:

- *Patience.* You just might not get what you want straight away!
- *Acceptance.* The kind you need to show your horse when you just know he's done the best he can on that day.
- *Goal setting.* Learning to achieve long term goals through daily small steps.
- *Social skills.* Not everyone you meet is going to be a great friend, but in a small barn community, you do learn to get along and compromise, especially when the horses are involved.
- *Dedication.* You quickly realize that you might not be able to get your horse to do what you want right away. Horse riders develop this tenacity that gets them through the difficult times – try, try again and give it another try the next time.

iii

- *Planning and Organization.* You need to plan on the fly (or rather, on the horse's back)! Think ahead for everything from the next scheduled lesson to the next part of your dressage test or the next part of the jump course. Not everything goes according to plan, but you surely do have to keep your ducks in a row when it comes to setting and meeting your goals.

- *Humility.* Riding horses teaches you one thing in particular, and probably quite quickly: you don't have the answer to everything, and you can be wrong – often! More importantly, you will learn that being wrong isn't so terrible and you'll just have to adjust your behavior the next ride.

- *Forgiveness.* Something that amazes me over and over again is how forgiving horses are. Even if you do make mistakes - and you will make more than you can imagine - they will be there the next day, ready and willing to give you another try. The key though is to not take it for granted, and give it your best effort to change whatever needs changing. And then, you will develop your capacity for forgiveness as well.

Once you go through these sorts of experiences (and there are many more than just those listed above), you will begin to recognize that horses do in fact, change you. They help elevate your character and your way of being.

Section 3: Life.

They change your life. There is no other way to put it.

In this third section of the book, you will read about the different ways people change when they begin interacting with horses. There are tips on how to care for horses, how to improve your level of communication from the ground, and all the reasons why we appreciate our horses so much.

Something about riding horses prompts us to work on our own mental aptitude and attitude. From the coordination of the aids to developing the elusive *feel* that comes along with riding, there are concepts in this book that will help you explore the hidden factors of riding – the ones you may not have time to really explore while you are on the horse's back. While practical, many of the riding tips are designed to help you synthesize the many factors that go into physical skill development.

As the years pass by, and you become a *horse* person, you will realize that horses (and riding) don't just impact your abilities – they impact your life. In the final section of the book, you will read about balance, your (horse) life path, perfection, and all that comes with living the life of horses.

I hope this third book of the *Horse Listening Collection* takes you on a similar reflective path as it did for me while I wrote it. Wishing you the best as you make horses and riding your life!

Section 1: Horses.

Because of Riding

She can drive through heavy traffic with the precision of knowing exactly which wheel is where in a given moment.

She knows just when to ask a little more and when she should back off.

She organizes her time effectively and multitasks like a pro!

She is a life-long learner.

Because of Showing

She can break down seemingly impossible responsibilities into small manageable steps.

She does her "homework" knowing that the extra effort usually pays off.

She perseveres especially when things get difficult.

Because of Horses

She knows communication is a two-way street and listens as often as she speaks.

She clearly reads your nonverbal body language.

She knows how to follow effectively but can also lead along with the best of them.

She knows when it's time to say goodbye.

1 Seven Ways to Listen to Your Horse

Listening to your horse is such an important part of riding and horse ownership. In fact, the rider who is ignorant of the messages her horse sends is missing out on sometimes vital information.

Knowing how to understand and correctly interpret the signs and behaviors of your horse allows you to know when something is off. The feedback you get from your horse can inform everything from general health care, to training and conditioning programs, to your horse's mental well-being.

How can you learn to listen effectively, in a way that positively affects your horse? Here are a some ideas.

1. Body Condition
When you become familiar with the way your horse looks, you will notice very small changes in your horse's body condition – even from one day to another. Does your horse's body look a little lean? Maybe it's time to increase hay or grain just a bit. Is your horse a bit roly-poly? Cut back! How

about when you notice super tight muscles? Maybe you'll be in for a bit of a wilder ride that day! Is the horse tucked in the flank area? That can be a warning for gut problems or some sort of discomfort. Consistently evaluate your horse's body condition to identify how he feels and what he needs – on a daily basis.

2. Herd Dynamics

Take a few minutes when you go to catch your horse, or alternately, when you turn him back out into the herd. How does he interact with his herd mates? Does he have any favorite pals that he spends time with regularly? How does he negotiate his way around the herd hierarchy?

Once you know what "normal" is, you will be able to tell when something just doesn't seem right. If your horse is usually a member of the crowd, finding him all alone at the back of the field might indicate that something is just not right.

3. Weather Conditions

Does your horse turn on his "inner stallion" when the temperature drops 20 degrees overnight? When you head to the barn, do you notice his that ample topline muscles dissolved overnight thanks to the chill in the air?

Then today might be the day that you should lunge him before you ride! (Trust me – I have the T-short on this one!) Or conversely, what happens to your horse with a 20 degree increase?

Does he want to have nothing to do with exercise while he's sweating just standing still? Maybe this is the day you hose him off after a shorter ride and leave him inside during the highest heat of the day.

4. Distractibility

Some days, your horse might want to do more "TV watching" than ride. Rather than respond to your aids, he's looking left/ right/ straight – focussing attention everywhere except where you want it! In this case, you might need to change your riding plans.

Do more "pop quizzes" and be more active in your own riding. Insist on more suppleness. Slow down his leg speed if he is running. Do something different to challenge him and get his attention.

5. Body Language

Horses rely mainly on body language to communicate with each other. The signals are fairly consistent among all horses, so if you can learn to understand the behaviors, you will know exactly where you stand in your mini-herd of two.

For example, if you approach your horse and he turns his head away, you know that he isn't completely comfortable with your approach. When you notice him getting out of your space, step back and invite him back.

Given enough repetition and time, your horse will learn first, that you have no aggressive intentions when you walk up to him, and second, that he can step into your personal space. This fairly simple exchange develops your horse's trust in you.

6. While Riding

After you ride the same horse for a while, you get to know how he feels under regular conditions. So if one day you get on, and all you get is tail swishes or reluctance to move forward, you know this is a sign that he isn't quite right. Maybe your gelding was running around in the field yesterday and is muscle sore now. Or maybe your mare is in heat and not able to move as well as usual.

Regardless of the reason, there is no need to push a horse that you know would normally be forward moving and willing. Always consider unusual discomfort as a sign to look into the horse's physical (or mental) needs.

7. Eating Habits

What are your horse's normal eating patterns? Does he wolf his feed down, or does he pick daintily at each and every oat kernel? It is important for you to know these things, because a change in eating behavior is a huge indicator of other impending problems.

When you notice something abnormal, be ready to analyze everything from the feed itself to the horse's physical health and mental well-being. Narrow it down by starting with the most obvious first. These signs are only a few ways that you can learn to "listen" to your horse. The more time you can invest into getting to know your horse, and the more you can educate yourself about riding, horse health and body language, the more you will be able to almost literally understand about your horse.

The concept of "horse listening" begins with the human. If we can improve our own knowledge and behavior, we will invariably be able to support our horses so they can be happy, healthy and active well into their old age.

2 A (Not So) Surprising Benefit of Horsin' Around - Regularly

This week, I learned once again all about the benefits of regular riding.

I have been making extra effort to spend enough time with the horses, whether while riding, or doing something in-hand, or even just grooming. I did something almost every day.

And so, I was scheduled to ride Cyrus today. But the weather had plans of its own. The stunningly beautiful sun-shiny morning morphed into cloud-covered, threatening-to-rain afternoon sky.

The cold front had met the warm front and we were suddenly in the middle of a weather-changing windstorm. Trees leaned left and right. Leaves flew first up ever so high, before landing on the grass.

A dark puff of cloud headed over the riding ring, threatening rain.

Undeterred, I thought I'd give it a good go. If nothing else, I'd give us a chance to squeeze in a quick workout – either in saddle or not – and call it a day. I put my imaginary bubble around us and got into the saddle. As Cyrus sauntered off into a calm, soft walk, I knew I'd be able to ride today.

I expected Cyrus to spook.

I expected him to get all excited, to throw in a buck or a sidestep in response to the sound of the gusts as they whistled in our ears.

I expected him to move with tension, jigging the walk or bracing the back. Instead, he was the picture of reliability. We walked, trotted and cantered without one false step.

Turn left? OK. Canter right? No problem. Work on the pattern? What fun!

Once again, I was reminded how horses, like humans, enjoy attention.

The more I do with Cyrus, the more he wants to do. So today, although I could see the weather approaching, I didn't want to leave without a quick ride. And I was rewarded with such a great time!

I guess it goes without saying that the more we do, the better the horses become. We already know that every major goal begins with a first small step. Even if a single ride doesn't go as well as we'd hoped, each ride adds up. Assuming we follow a set plan with a sound lesson and training strategy, we can make progress step by step, day by day.

Today's fantastic ride was a delightful surprise and made me realize yet again how important it is to find a regular riding routine. Stick with the plan, and give it all you've got! Because the horses are truly worth it.

3 Do You Want to Own a Horse?

You think you have everything in place to take the plunge.

Horse ownership is replete with dream-come-true moments, physical activity the likes of which is not provided by any other sport, and the sheer beauty of the magnificent animal that you can feel permanently attached to.

People often become lifelong horse owners and learn how to manage and maintain their lives in order to provide adequately for their horses. But in many cases, what begins as a fulfilled fantasy ends in a disastrous situation – perhaps for the owner, but more importantly, for the voiceless horse that is dependent on human care.

Although it may seem easy to leave a horse at a boarding barn that is managed by someone else, there are still other factors that can come into play that might make or break your ownership experience. Sometimes, what seems at first as a small inconvenience can turn into *the* deal-breaker.

Take a look at the questions below to see how many you can answer "yes" to. All of them are important factors in horse ownership.

Do you have time?

If you think lack of time at the barn might be a factor, then hold back from committing to horse ownership. Horses take time – to groom, to clean tack, to feed and turn in/out if you are going to care for them yourself. They want time for attention, handling, training. They thrive on routine, including regular riding. If you think you might have trouble getting to the barn several times a week, consider other options.

Do you have a fair amount of experience?

At some point, most of us were complete strangers to horses and the horsey lifestyle. Although we probably recognized a strong affinity right from the beginning, learning about the ways of horses takes several years of regular exposure and consistent feedback from someone who is willing to train *you*.

Someone new to horses might unknowingly live the adage: "a little knowledge can be a dangerous thing." Many people bite off more than they can chew, especially in the early years, simply because of lack of experience.

If you are still developing your skills, take another route. Try part-boarding someone's horse so you can learn as you go.

Do you have patience to spare?

Horse riding and training takes a lot of patience! At times, you must be willing to try again and again, and be satisfied with one step forward, two steps back. You will learn quickly that there is no replacement to consistency and that especially in horseback riding, there is no such thing as instant gratification.

There is an old horsey truth that the horse is the mirror of the rider. You must know before you step into commitment that the horse will only be able to do as much as you can, regardless of his previous training level. However, you can be sure that he will improve as you improve – and there is no shortcut!

Are you responsible?

You can count on one thing: problems will come up. For example, there may be unplanned injuries, when the horse ends up being unrideable for weeks on end.

You will still have to pay for board and increase the level of daily care. Whatever happens, you have to always keep your horse in mind and be ready to be the "go to" person.

Is it more than just about how cute they are?

Yes, horses have historically been revered for their magnificence and enduring beauty. Watching a horse perform at his potential is an awe-inspiring moment, even at a basic level show or demonstration. Being witness to the power and grace of a rambunctious horse as he plays with his pasture mates can become a lasting memory. But none of the above should be the entire reason for purchasing a horse.

Are you humble and empathetic?

Some people seem to ride only to demonstrate their strength and superiority over such a huge animal. There is probably going to be a time to assert yourself, especially if you find yourself in a dangerous situation. However, if you want to constantly impose your desires on a horse regardless of the horse's level of ability or if you feel offended when the horse doesn't comply to your requests, then horse ownership is definitely not for you.

Do you have a mentor?

Even if you have spent several years learning from the other people and their horses, you will do well to find yourself someone who is willing to help you figure out your horse, especially in the first few years. There is nothing worse than having to address problems for the first time without having the background or someone's help. Having a mentor can make all the difference in your success as a new horse owner.

Good horse keeping is a life-long pursuit, and you learn something new from every horse you come across. It has been said that there is a horse somewhere that humbles every rider. You need to be able to separate the ego from the event and be willing to give it another try another day. Just like people, horses have good days and bad days. Know when to let it go.

Can you afford it?

It certainly is true that horse keeping is very expensive. Either you have to pay someone to provide care, feed, bedding and shelter for you, or you have to do it all yourself. After the basic requirements, you will most likely need to budget for riding lessons at the least, or horse training by a professional if your horse is young or needs additional training. Add to that vet bills, supplements and show costs, and you will have a good idea of the financial commitment you are making. Plan out all of this ahead of time!

What can you do if you don't own a horse?

The possibilities are endless:

- *take regular riding lessons* to see if you can maintain a consistent riding schedule. Learn the basic skills of riding, and wait until such time that you have ridden several different horses of different types and temperaments, so you know what style of riding you like and what the ideal personality of your horse should be.

- *ride someone else's horse.* You might be lucky enough to find a horse owner who is happy to share their horse with you at no cost, especially if you are fairly experienced and can improve their horse's training in the process.

- *part-board a horse* and share in the wonderful experience of horse ownership without actually owning the horse. When part-boarding, you will discover what it is like to be part of a barn community and develop the experience necessary to know what to do during specific situations. You can always turn to the horse's owner to learn how to deal with horse health concerns and training problems that you might not otherwise be able to solve on your own.

- *take on a full lease.* Choose to take on a full lease if you want to be the primary rider of a horse, but you don't want to be responsible for the horse over its entire lifetime. Many owners are happy to lease their horse to someone who will incur the costs of keeping the horse and provide the regular exercise that the horse needs, even if only for a year or two.

Once you make the decision to take on the full care and responsibility of a horse, be ready to make real and significant changes to your lifestyle. Knowing what the possible difficulties might be ahead of time will enable you to make the best, most informed decision, and will likely predict the success of your endeavor!

4 Top 8 Perks of Horse Keeping

Keeping horses at your own place can be a daunting task. Going out in freezing/hot and humid/pouring rain/ snow storm weather is not for everyone. Early mornings and late nights, staying home when others go out/on vacation/sleep in (occasionally) can be enough to keep most people far away from barn management.

The work is physical and thankless and it MUST be done regardless of your mood or health condition, because the horses depend on it.

So, in contrast to all the negatives, here are a few positives that keep us going when everyone else is enjoying their leisure time.

8. Feeling the "bright and early" (in the dark of winter) crispy air freshness drag you out of your first-thing-in-the-morning-sluggishness before even the birds start chirping!

7. Hearing the soft, encouraging "Welcome! Now get our breakfast going" nickers as you walk in the barn.

6. Hanging on to the lead rope, speed-walking beside the bright-eyed, perky-eared, energetic horse on a mission to the paddock – every day is a new discovery!

5. Listening to contented munching sounds mixed with occasional heartfelt snorts as the horses start on their hay breakfasts.

4. Getting a chance to "read" the stalls to know how your horse spent the night and is feeling in the morning.

3. Knowing what is fed and when it is fed – no arguments/negotiations to deal with about the feed you want your horse to have!

2. Being at the barn at least twice a day makes for an easy "check" to make sure all is well with the horses, and a good excuse to ride since you're already there.

1. No gym membership needed – especially after moving the hay bales and mucking stalls (strength training), walking back and forth to and from the paddocks (cardio training), interspersed with wheelbarrow dumps (interval training). It's all covered each and every day!

5 Speaking Horse (A.K.A. Pushing the Envelope)

You've seen it before (maybe you've been there yourself?) – the horse/human tug-of-war scenario:

The person is trying desperately to keep the horse in a particular position
- or -
the person is leading the horse somewhere and all the while, the horse is moving, imposing, and once in a while, running over the doting human being!

Once you know how to listen to your horse, a whole world of communication can open up for you. You will know how to interpret what the horse is saying – to the other horses, to you, and to the 'world'. Horses send messages out as much as humans do. It's just that we do it verbally (just think of what a gathering of people sounds like and you'll know what I mean).

Horses, on the other hand, do very little verbally (unless the horses belong to me – they've definitely learned to 'voice' their opinion).

Most of their communication lies in the non-verbal realm; you need to learn to 'listen' in a different sense, by carefully observing their body movements. Pretty much *every* movement has a meaning and is 'sent out' with deliberate intention. The talent on your part is to interpret the body language accurately.

Point in fact – the horse's social structure works on a basic hierarchical system. Lower-level horses always defer to the herd leader. In other words, if the herd leader moves into the direction of another horse, the lower horse is expected to move away – from the hay, from another horse friend, or simply from the herd leader himself.

Neglecting to move away often results in a more aggressive movement from the herd leader – including the possibility of a swift kick in the lower-level horse's direction!

This submission has developed over the millennia for good reason – the herd leader *had* to be the one who moved the herd around. In nature, without a good leader to tell the others what to do and where to go, the herd's safety would be at risk.

How does this involve you, the human? Your actions will dictate your current and future relationship with that horse. Here is a possible scenario: while you are leading the horse beside you, the horse steps into your direction, almost walking on top of you. Your possible responses:

– you think it's cute that the horse wants to snuggle up to you, and you step back as the horse walks into you

– you see the horse coming in your direction and you push the horse on his shoulder so he doesn't continue coming into your space

Each reaction on your part gives the horse a different message. The first reaction – stepping away – will tell the horse that he is the herd leader between the two of you, and that he should be the one to make decisions. Many times, this 'herd dynamic' works just fine for your interactions, because chances are that your horse is kind and generous and usually will not be inclined toward stepping on you or dragging the lead rope out of your hand.

But unfortunately, the one time that he feels he must impose his authority on you (if he feels threatened by an unfamiliar object), you will not have a say in his decision-making. As the lower ranked member of your herd, you must obey – meaning, you'd better get out of his way as he tramples you to get away from the fear object!

If instead, you choose to not move away and push him back out of your space the moment you notice him stepping toward you, you impart a very different message. In this case, you are telling him that you are the herd leader, and he needs to respect your personal space.

This is the preferable role for you as human, since you are likely more than six times smaller and lighter and at risk of being easily injured based on just the size difference itself.

As you learn to listen to your horse, you will realize that there is constant communication going back and forth between the two of you (whether you know it or not). So instead of assuming the subservient role, pay closer attention and work on asking your horse the questions. If you move into his space, will he move away from you? If you need him to stop moving his feet, will he stand still?

Make a habit of routinely asking him questions. If he answers "yes" to your questions, you can be thankful and reward him with a pat and a "good boy" vocal response, but your job is not quite complete. Just getting an affirmative is not enough – as soon as your horse gives you the 'yes', you need to ask him the next level of question.

Maybe it could be something like: "Will you stand still and not dive for the grass while I lead you in the field with the yummiest grass?" The next level might be, "Will you walk nicely and not prance around while I lead you away from the barn and your herd members?"

Each time you get the 'yes', think of something that could be the next step. Pushing the envelope is one step in developing a trusting, confident relationship with your horse.

What are some questions you ask of your horse?

6 Why Black and White is Better Than Gray

As a colour, gray gives variance to the spectrum between black and white. But with horses, "being" gray leaves too much unsaid, too many questions, too many options to choose from.

I'll tell you why gray doesn't work.

Gray Is
– wishy-washy
– unclear
– muddy
– unsure
– insecure
– confusing

Gray is simply too much in the middle.

Horses
– do better with a straight yes or no

– want all the wrong options eliminated
– gain confidence from a confident rider
– prefer a confident, secure leader

It is true that horses are constantly communicating with you. Through their physical interactions, they ask questions and answer yours. This regular interaction is the foundation of your training program. One of the most critical personal attributes a good rider has is clarity of aids and requests.

Often, the horses that find leader-humans are the happiest, most content horses to ride. They can rely on their partner to be clear, concise and sure. There is no guesswork required of the horse.

So how does this impact your regular riding routine?

Be Black and White in Riding

If you ask for a canter, get that canter. Don't let the horse trot away faster and faster until you finally just pull him up. If he trots off, slow the trot, ask for the canter again. Repeat. Be clear. Be concise. Maybe you need to re-establish the inside bend. Correct a dropped shoulder and then ask again.

If you asked for a turn, follow through when the horse drifts to the outside. Catch the horse's outside shoulder with the rein, use your outside leg to encourage better straightness from the rib cage, and encourage more impulsion from the hind end with your seat and leg aids.

23

Timeliness is the key when it comes to clarity. Don't wait ten, twenty, thirty or more strides before following through on your request. The quicker you can respond, the easier it will be for your horse to make connections.

If your horse needs to do something more basic, change the plan. But be specific in your intentions and reinforce/review/change the approach as required.

Stick to your program.

Be an active rider.

7 Five Common Horse and Riding Myths

Do you regularly find yourself explaining/ educating/ justifying/ rationalizing/defending your "horse habit"?
Do your parents/friends/co-workers/brother's children mock your passion and belittle the time, energy and effort you put into your beloved equine? Then this chapter is for you!

Although (from personal experience) it is usually very difficult to teach an skeptical person the method behind the equine madness, perhaps a little list outlining the most commonly-held falsehoods will begin to point them in the right direction!

1. Horse riding is for the rich.
How many people do you know who worked their way to one riding lesson a week? Some of us cleaned tack, scooped poop, groomed and tacked up horses for other riders! Then, some of us who bought horses into adulthood did so with careful budgeting plans, sharing our horses through part-boards and maybe even giving up on our own

personal comforts to find the most affordable boarding situations we could find.

It is true that the bill on horse maintenance can be limitless depending on what you want, but look carefully and you will find many average earners with average jobs with above-average passion for equines.

2. Horseback riding is easy.

I'm going to cut to the chase and say it: horseback riding is *not* easy. Just getting on, allowing an animal six times our size dictate where we go when and coordinating the body sufficiently to not fall off is enough of a feat in itself.

Making it *look* easy is even more of a challenge, and most of us spend our entire riding lives perfecting our skills to do just that. The riders who appear as if they are just floating along while the horse does all the work are precisely the ones who are busting a gut and sweating behind the scenes.

3. Horses require very little care.

It is true that horses can be left to fend for themselves and possibly even thrive in a grassy pasture. But watch and learn over a few seasons to discover that at the minimum, the pasture needs maintenance. The horses need fresh water and grooming. Once the pasture dries out/runs out/grows over, the horses will soon need hay supplemented to their grazing area.

Add to that any expectation for performance, and you will notice that the horse will need regular handling and training, better grooming, improved feed for a more balanced nutrition and better overall general health care and worming. Showing adds even more requirements: a regular vaccination and general health schedule, a higher quality of muscling and sheen to the coat, neater tails and manes and better behavior.

Committing to caring for and riding horses is not a task to be taken lightly. It does add up in time!

4. Horses are like dogs but bigger.

This one takes very little time to figure out. Horses are prey animals and dogs are predators. Aside from being companions to humans, they are on opposite ends of the spectrum in terms of social dynamics and behavior. As prey animals, horses have a highly developed flight or fight instinct (mostly flight in our domesticated horses) and tend to be resistant to hanging around long enough to make detailed observations about a threatening situation.

Horses respond differently to humans as leaders and communicate on a completely distinct level from dogs. Long-time dog owners switching over to horse ownership discover quickly that the cuddling, food-rewarded training techniques used on their dogs don't go very far on their horses. Soon enough, if they listen carefully, they learn a whole new language reserved especially for their equines!

5. Horses "love" people like we love them.
It takes time to learn to accurately interpret equine communication. What we think of as developing a loving attachment might not be exactly how the horse interprets it. Perhaps he connects with you because you have spent years developing a communication system that he is familiar and comfortable with. Perhaps he nickers and turns in your direction because he knows you will be feeding him shortly after your arrival to the barn!

Although so many books and movies have portrayed undying bonds between horses and their humans, don't be too disappointed if you begin to understand that the horse merely expects you to be another herd member! This is true and right and simply the way of the horse.

8 Eight Ways to Help Your Horse Achieve His Highest Potential

There are so many things we want to do with our horses! Some of us want to ride the trails. Some want to take lessons and progress in our skill levels. Others want to compete – in a manner of so many various disciplines that it is hard to list them all. Perhaps we want to work the horse from the ground, developing connection and communication at a level that is very different from human speech.

Regardless of what we want to *do* with our horses, our first responsibility is always to the horse. Before we can step into that stirrup, before we can work on developing that slide and before we ever can imagine heading to our local/regional/provincial (state)/national or international championships, we must be sure to meet the horse's needs.

The concept of "it depends" is the key to determining how much of what is necessary, how much is too little and how much is too much. One horse's "perfect" can be another horse's mental stress. What works for one doesn't work for another, and it does us well to learn to listen to our horses to develop an excellent management system that meets his particular needs.

Here are eight considerations to prepare your horse to be his best. Because *all* "performance" is based on the horse's health and mental well-being.

1. Feed Program

While it is true that some horses can get by perfectly well on hay in the winter and grass in the summer, once we introduce a workload to their regular regiment, it becomes necessary to examine the nutritional content of the feed program.

What you feed your horse is probably one of the most critical concerns. The more competitive, or demanding, his work gets, the more attention you need to give to his feed program. How much hay does he need? What sort of nutrition is necessary for the type of work he is doing? Will the requirements change as his work becomes more challenging?

2. Turn In

When we want the horses to perform, we should be cognizant of how much rest the horse needs. While many horses can do just fine in a completely outdoor environment, once you pass a certain level of exercise, the horse needs more care and attention to perform at his best.

Some horses will be required to maintain a top level coat condition and grooming. Some activities will require a fully rested, energetic horse that was guaranteed his sleep the night before. Some horses will need to stay inside, out of the elements in order to maintain the soft, supple topline that is needed for them to do their best.

3. Turn Out

Giving horses a chance to be out in the open air is as important as it is to give a horse inside time. Every horse benefits from time in the field or paddock, roaming free and having a chance to interact with his equine friends. Time outside stimulates the horse physically and mentally.

So there must always be an effective balancing act that combines time inside as well as outside, as required by the discipline and level of activity. Trial and error and experience will help you discover what combination works the best for your horse at his current state.

4. Health Care – Worming, Feet, Teeth, Routine Medical Care

It goes without saying that a horse has to be healthy before he can perform at his best. When left to the wayside, any of the above considerations may impact the horse's level of achievement. At large boarding barns, the barn manager may maintain a regular schedule for all the horses. At smaller, more private environments, it falls to the owner to maintain regular shots, foot care, teeth floating and worming program.

5. Physical/Mental Stimulation

Over thousands of years, horses have lived their lives travelling, carrying, pulling and being ridden. Although horses can be quite content living out their lives in a pasture, most horses benefit physically and mentally from movement and stimulation.

The more you challenge the horse, the better he may feel about his surroundings, his people and his life. Good movement feels good to the horse, and he will let you know!

6. Blanketing

Some people feel that blankets should never be used on horses. However, a blanket can be a horse's "portable shelter". When can a horse use a blanket? If the bugs are strong enough to bite welts into his skin, make him pace all day until dark, or lose half of his tail hairs from all that swishing.

Similarly, the horse that trembles in the cold rain or does not develop an adequate winter coat can benefit from additional covering during the winter months. Using a blanket might result in a distinct improvement in your horse's coat quality, enhancing cleanliness and overall sheen.

7. Feel Good Rides

Learn how to make your horse move well and you might be surprised at how much he enjoys his exercise! If you can make him happy, your horse will eagerly enjoy his riding sessions.

8. Be the Best Rider/Trainer You Can Be

Well, you are part of the equation as well. If you continue to be a life-long learner, developing your skills over the long term, you can become a huge asset to any horse you ride. Take lessons in your area of choice, develop your skills and become an active and effective rider in the partnership with your horse.

9 Six Reasons to Thank My Horses

Horses have given to us in so many ways that it can become difficult to measure their contribution to humanity. In history, horses were literally beasts of burden, walking beside or carrying people to their successes as societies and civilizations. These days, horses have been relegated to a perhaps more simple life as either livestock or recreational pets, once again dependent on their human counterparts for their safety and relevance in society.

On a more personal level, horses continue to contribute to our lives in very specific and measurable ways. Here are six reasons why I thank my horses for their impact on my life.

1. Self-Development
I'm not sure if I was a life-long learner before I ever rode, or if horse riding has made me into a life-long learner. Regardless, there is no doubt that you will never finish learning how to ride.

There are infinite levels of pretty much every skill and idea that goes into riding, and just when you think you know it all, your horse calmly throws you a new curve that makes you dig into the depths of your character and come up with something you had never realized to that point. Yes, it is true that horses help us humans develop humility and selflessness.

2. Exercise and Athletic Growth

Without a doubt, riding keeps you active, flexible and vibrant. The horses keep me heading to the great outdoors even in the direst of weather conditions, if only to make sure that they are comfortable, fed and warm/cool as required by the season. Regular riding also plays an important part in developing and maintaining my level of activity – and the best part is that the better I get at riding, the more fine-tuned my body needs to become to respond even better to the horse's movements.

3. Generosity of Spirit

Day after day and ride after ride, I marvel at the horses that allow us to share in their strength and presence through riding. Not only do they carry us and go left and right as commanded, but they also often become partners in movement and do their best to respond to our sometimes unclear or ineffective aids.

4. Keeping Me Grounded

Although there is most definitely the aura of excessive-ness (and expensive-ness) surrounding the riding or owning of horses, it is ironically the horses that keep me earth-bound and in my place.

For if you have the opportunity to care for the horses, and put some sweat (and sometimes tears) into their upkeep and maintenance, you will know what it means to be one person just doing what needs to be done without the expectation of any reward other than just meeting everyone's needs.

5. Making Friends

One thing I know is that no matter where I go, I can find and make friends in the horse world. I think that despite our differences of style and discipline, all horse people share one common interest – the horse. Many of my closest and longest lasting friendships originally began at some horse event, barn or activity. Thanks to the horses, I have friends of all ages and from all over the country – and my social life is full of get-togethers with horsey friends.

6. Beauty and Grace

Maybe you're like me when it comes to horses. To this day, I am captivated every time a horse kicks up his heels, arches his neck and gallops off into a joyful celebration of life. My 32-year-old Kayla still marches out to the field with a spark in her eyes and a bounce to her (very long) strides that reminds me every day of this beautiful and remarkable thing we call life.

Horses give us opportunities for experiences and growth that are not part of everyday urban living. I, for one, am always aware of the gifts that horses have given to me over the years. There is so much to be thankful for.

Section 2: Riding.

10 When Do You Start Riding Your Horse?

"When do you start riding your horse?"
This question was being posed to me by a very respected and horse-wise mentor one day long ago, early in my riding development.

I thought about it for some time, and responded, "When I lead the horse to the riding ring." During the time I'm leading the horse to the ring, I usually start mentally running through my goals for the day. I quickly review my last ride and think of the small "next steps" I'm going to address.

She stopped me in my tracks.

"That's already too late," she said.

———————————————————

These words have stayed with me to this very day. She emphasized that "riding" is not limited to just being on the horse's back.

Whether you are leading a horse from or to the paddock, grooming, or just playing in the round pen, you are "riding". Riding a horse is about *everything*!

The truth about horses is that they do not differentiate between riding and handling and just plain socializing. In their world, every contact you have with them is first about herd dynamics.

Whether you like it or not, or know it or not, your horse is in vigorous conversation with you from moment you start interacting with him. And the dominant question in his mind is, "Are you a leader?"

Your physical responses then point him to his answer.

How to be a leader
1. Attitude matters. Be sure in your step. Know where you are going, and kindly but firmly expect the horse to come along with you.

2. Establish your "personal space." In the herd, horses regularly test each other's boundaries by pushing into personal space. While you lead your horse, feed him or groom him, be aware of the slight tests your horse puts you through.

3. "Test" your horse. Always ask questions of your horse. Will you put a foot here? Will you get out of my space? Will you let me give your head a long and squishy hug?

4. Always follow through with your requests. If you happen to get a "no" for an answer (it does happen all the time!), you have to be ready to continue that particular conversation until you get the "yes". If you accept the first "no", then the next and the next, you will be sabotaging your relationship with your horse. And he will know it before you do.

My mentor looked at me squarely. I realized then that she had *known* what my answer was going to be all along. She wanted to make sure that I understood clearly about the horse-human relationship.

I hesitantly asked her, "When do you start riding your horse?"

Her answer: "When I pull into the driveway."

11 On Being the Perpetual Riding Student, Mastery and the Time Warp!

As horseback riders, it helps a whole lot if we are content to be forever students.

We are continually floating around in this perpetual learning curve. Just as you think you've got something down for real, other things pop up – and you find yourself back at square one, even if you're relearning something for the hundredth time.

The catch is that there are so many levels of learning of any one aspect of riding.

Take transitions, for example. First off, you think that a good transition consists of a horse actually changing gait after you use your aids. Then, you realize that a good transition happens at a determined location – so it's no longer good enough to get just the gait change.

After you become more precise, you realize that a good transition happens where you want it *and* that it should be well-balanced. So you work hard on getting your horse to use his hind end and your half-halts help him stay off his forehand even though he might be doing a downward transition.

Once you get your balanced transition at your desired location, you realize that a good transition happens where you want it, in balance and more! Now you've discovered the great feeling of "forward"– the energy should flow freely from the back to the front of the horse!

Then you figure out that a precise, balanced, forward transition happens from the seat. So you work hard at using your core muscles and seat and legs in place of your hands. But later on, your good transition must also include a light use of aids. You spend time on developing even better communication with your horse so that you can soften all your aids and still get the balanced, forward gait change.

And so it goes on and on. Nothing we do in riding has an end to it. I'm sure you can think of other stages of what could be considered as a "good" transition.

This is where being life-long learner comes into play!

The good news is that the more you learn, the more you know coming into a new situation.

The bad news is that every time you learn something new, what you *thought* you already had mastered changes!

Sometimes, the new learning adds to what you have been doing so far. Other times, you might have to rework your whole understanding!

In my experience as a rider and instructor, you can break down pretty much all of our learning into four phases.

Phase 1: Coordination and Aids

The first phase usually takes quite a bit of both physical and mental effort. Everything seems new. You develop "feels" that you haven't known. You find you have to put quite a bit of attention into learning the aids, developing coordination of the aids, and figuring out the timing in relation to the horse's gaits. There is little for you to refer to in terms of background knowledge or experience, so you might not even know what you are looking for!

At first, it seems like you are doing way too much. Hand here, leg there, seat bone here... there are many bits and pieces that go into to creating a successful whole movement and because you are new to the movements, it takes thought and focus to put everything in its place.

Somewhere in the middle, you might feel like there is no way you're going to get it. You *think* you are doing the right thing, but the horse is not responding the way he should.

You might wonder that your instructor is asking too much of you. There might be confusion, difficulty in understanding the why and the what. You might get frustrated and sometimes even want to give up (this is when it's as healthy for you to quit as it is for your horse) – well, just for that day, of course!

But then at some point, something different happens.

Phase 2: The Time Warp

This happened to me one of the first times that everything seemed to fall together. After getting used to trying, doing, keep on going, never stopping… a light bulb moment happened without any intention on my part. Suddenly, I found all this extra time while everything that was supposed to happen, simply happened on its own! What used to take 5 seconds seemingly happened with little effort in 1.

I call it the "Time Warp" because it almost feels like time stands still. Everything happens together, fluidly, in coordination, and you get to just sit there while it all happens. Has something like this ever happened to you?

I believe that this feeling is the in-between stage of the initial struggle of learning, and the final mastery. So when you hit the Time Warp (or however you want to think of it), you know you've finally put together all the aids in a way that makes sense for your horse.

Phase 3: Mastery

Mastery happens when you can duplicate the skills repeatedly under different circumstances.

Let's use the transition example, at the first level of understanding. If you can get your horse to consistently make a change gaits after you've applied the aids, you're on your way to mastering the first level of transitions. If you can get different horses doing the same thing, you've really mastered that skill!

Mastery is great because you know what to do, when, where and why, and you can reproduce it at will. The effect is almost instantaneous and your horse feels *better* after you've applied your aids. You've finally arrived!

Phase 4: The Next Level

That is, until you notice that next level. You might become aware of it on your own, or your instructor might give you a push in the direction. In any case, you realize that there is so much more to that one skill.

For example, doing the transition just anywhere suddenly doesn't become good enough for you. Now, you want to do it at a particular spot!

The only catch – you start the learning process all over at Phase 1. *Aaaand* you go through the rest of the phases, then discover the new next level, and repeat the cycle again and again and again and again....

12 How Do You Develop "Feel" In Horseback Riding?

By three methods we may learn wisdom:
First, by reflection, which is noblest;
Second, by imitation, which is easiest;
and third by experience, which is the bitterest.
~Confucius

Confucius might well have been writing about "feel" in his quote above. Just replace the word 'wisdom' with 'feel' and you will get a generally good idea of the path.

Born to feel?

Many people say that it is impossible to learn how to 'feel' in riding. They say either you have it, or you don't. They insist that people who can 'feel' are essentially born with it, and others will never find it regardless of their attempts.

But you know this cannot possibly be true. You have likely watched as people improved their riding skills over time and witnessed for yourself that (correct) practice *does* make perfect (or at the very least, significant improvement).

Of course, certain requirements have to be in place:
– you need regular instruction.
– you must commit to consistent practice.
– you must be willing to hear and respond to repeated feedback.
– you must have the intrinsic motivation to strive for more at all times.

Most importantly, you need to have the openness of heart and mind to 'find' that feel – especially during the first time, since you will not particularly know what the feel *feels* like!

How to find 'feel'?
Do like Confucius said!

First, you must start with an idea. Before you will even know what to feel for, you must get some input from a more experienced source. Perhaps you have an instructor that puts emphasis on describing the feel for you. Maybe you can read about the feel from an expertly written book or article.

The difficulty about this stage is that *you don't know what you don't know…* and to break the cycle, you need to reach out to someone who does know. The road to knowing (or feeling, in this case), is *trusting* that there is something "out there" that you don't even know exists! Then you need the teaser idea to get you started, to start (figuratively) groping around to find that feel.

Second, watch, learn and do. There is no learning that is more successful than having a chance to watch someone ride, and then trying it yourself. *Imitate!* Ideally, you would be able to ride in the company of other experienced riders and try to mimic their actions.

Even better, ride with your instructor and listen to her as she explains what she is doing, what she is feeling, and what the end result looks like in the horse.

Then it is your turn to try and search for the feeling that will produce the final result. Unfortunately, you will have to get it wrong many times before you get the first taste of correct feel. At long last, after your instructor explained the skills, and then the feel, you might get a brief moment when it all falls together – and you *feel!*

Then, it all falls apart again!

Now you need to develop experience. After you get it that one time, you might not get it again for a while. You have to trouble-shoot – hit and miss – until you find the feel the second time. Each time, it gets easier to repeat, and you can duplicate the feel sooner and more frequently.

Sometimes, you will go through a stage where you simply cannot reproduce the feel (and result) without your instructor's steady guidance from the ground. You might be successful for the last twenty minutes of the lesson, but not be able to reproduce the skill on your own.

It *will* get worse before it gets better. As Confucius indicates, learning through experience can be "bitterest!"

Be patient. Getting to a point where the feel becomes part of your blueprint takes time and repetition. Persist through the uncoordinated moments, try again, and keep searching for that evasive feel. It really does get easier with time and practice.

If you can ride with feel, you will be able to respond immediately to your horse's needs, be able to avoid problems before they occur, and be present in the ride but out of your horse's way at the same time. And, to top it off, your horse will thank you for it!

13 Horseback Riders Do Nothing Anyway!

Well, at least, that's what "they" say. But *we* know differently, don't we?

We know how much time it takes to develop the balance and timing to move as a unit with the horse.

We know about the frustration and tears we expend when we work so hard to achieve something and still it does not arrive.

We know the pain we must go through – literally and figuratively – to develop enough "saddle time" to feel even the beginnings of unity and harmony with the horse.

It's like a picture.

Every time you watch a horse and rider, you are seeing where they are in their development as a partnership at that moment in time. Their strengths as well as their weaknesses are but a snapshot of their progress, a simple moment in time *after* where they have been and *before* where they are going.

The trick is to know that the picture they currently present is malleable and ever moving onward, like a flowing river.

The challenges they have right now are going to drift away with practice and new ones will take their places.

The unlimited potential for learning and self-development is the never-ending call of horseback riding.

To those who insist that the rider does nothing

When you see the rider that *looks like* she is "doing nothing", please be aware that:

- her timing is so well-developed that she is riding "in" the movement of the horse, intimately intertwined within his gait so as to dance into his rhythm.
- she is incredibly fit and strong through her core muscles, as well as self-aware of the balance and positioning of every cell of her body from tip of the head to the toes, so that the horse's movements do not lurch her out of the saddle.
- she knows when and how to allow the expression of the horse to come through and then capably rides along with him.
- she has developed a level of communication with her horse so sophisticated that it rivals the best, most successful social media platform known in existence to humankind!
- she has more dedication and self-discipline than many who are watching her.

In fact, us horseback riders are always in the hunt for *looking* like we are doing nothing at all! Because we know that an effortless, free-flowing, lighter-than-air ride truly *is* what we're aiming for…

…and we do not really mind if those onlookers think we are just being passengers on a magnificent animal who is willing to share his talents with us!

14 Riding Is Simple, But Not Easy!

It's Simple!

As riders, we become inspired and motivated while watching the equestrian disciplines during the Olympics.

Hold your breath as the cross-country eventers fly high over the step-up jumps that conceal what lays beyond. Marvel at the tight turns that the jumper horses make on their approach to higher-than-your-head-height poles and proceed to launch their great bodies over. Be amazed at the almost imperceptible communication displayed by the dressage horses and their riders as they literally dance across the ring with grace and gravity-defying strength.

Yet, back at the ranch, we find ourselves frustrated that we are having difficulty communicating one thing or another, or feeling hopeless that something will never come together.

It's complicated!

It is precisely during these moments that we have to keep in mind the true depth of what we are trying to achieve with the horse.

Let's face it – *all* we want is for the horse to do what we want, when we want, where we want, with suppleness and strength!

When it comes down to it, if you truly understand how those Olympic riders perform (at such high levels of achievement in tandem with their incredible four-legged partners), you know what you are watching is akin to a small miracle.

Everything has to come together at the right time.

To the onlooker, it all looks so easy.
Yes, the good riders make it seem effortless.

But take a closer look, and you will notice the sweat dripping from their brows, their lungs heaving as they regulate their breath post-performance, and their own wonderment as they realize that their goals have become reality.

Now try it yourself!
It is definitely not as easy as it looks.

After some riding experience with our own horses, we begin to realize that riding can be complicated. We discover that the horse has his own motivations, abilities, desires and work ethic. No matter how you slice it, as riders, we have to work *with* our horses, developing their weaknesses, playing with their strengths, keeping them happy and enthusiastic.

You know you are on the right track when things become difficult. The more you develop your ability to communicate effectively to the horse through your body, the more complicated the technical aspects become.

This is where you develop a deeper understanding of the chasm of difference between "simple" and "easy". Yes, it is *simple* to get a horse to move in an uphill manner, but maybe not as *easy* as you may have originally thought!

Where do you stand on the "easy" vs. "simple" concept?

15 Ten Habits of Competent Riders

We can all think of a rider we know that seems to always do well, has calm, happy horses, and steadily improves their horse's physical and mental state in an almost effortless manner.

We watch and admire from afar, but in fact, we can all stand to learn from their regular habits and "way of being" in order to develop our own horse riding mantra.

What do great riders have in common that makes them appealing to watch, steadily develop their riding skills and become role models for others to aspire to emulate?

1. Persistence: Good riders are willing to try, try again. They know that there will be more rides, more days, and the slow and steady approach always wins the "race".

2. Open-mindedness: Good riders know there is something to be learned from everyone, even if to see proof of why *not* to do something. These riders are not discipline exclusive, and are always aware that good riding is good riding is good riding, regardless of the saddle or style.

3. Patience: Good riders are willing to wait to reap the rewards. They know that even if something falls apart today, there will be more days to come and small steps even backward are more beneficial than quick fixes or shortcuts.

4. Quitting: This may seem counter-intuitive, but good riders quit while they're ahead. They ride for short periods of time to their highest ability and then call it a day. They seem to intuitively know when enough is enough.

5. Effectiveness: Good riders seek maximum effectiveness with minimum harm. They make every step count, and they resist overriding the horse for the sake of performance.

6. Self-Improvement: Good riders regularly seek to upgrade their riding skills and general horse education. They are willing to spend time, money and humility in the quest for constant self-improvement.

7. Seeing the Big Picture: Good riders enjoy the "work" and the path as much as they do the goal achievement. They know that each day and each step is as important as the other and is a natural progression in development.

8. Role Models: Good riders know good riding when they see it and seek to surround themselves with those who will not only help them improve on a riding level, but also on a more personal and inspirational level as well.

9. Problem Solving: Good riders can trouble-shoot through problems to come to gratifying solutions. They have many tools in their "tool-boxes" and know there is more than one way to approach a situation. They are always willing to try new things.

10: Horse Listeners: Good riders are expert horse listeners! They are sensitive to the feedback from their horses and adjust their responses accordingly.

It's as simple as that!

16 What You Ought to Know About Instant Gratification

As you become a better rider, you begin to run into obstacles that were previously unnoticeable. Invariably, there comes a time when the simple becomes complicated. Without warning, riding becomes more than just the various gaits and transitions, more than a turn with the hands. You read and study and watch and discover that there is so much more to each gait, more to each turn, and more to the joys of riding.

The original walk that once felt adequate is no longer satisfying. That wonderful canter is now not quite balanced enough. You discover nerve endings where there were none before, and you are inspired to reach for new heights thanks to energizing "feels" emanating from an enthusiastic horse, confirming more than ever that you are on the right path.

The joy that went along with the simplicity of riding might be temporarily gone. You approach days of confusion, questions, and ultimately, frustration. You wonder why there seems to be so many details, so many little nuances that change sometimes on an even daily basis. And you begin to wonder:

Why is riding so difficult?

The quick and easy answer is that riding horses is about combining many and varied details into one – nothing can be achieved in isolation.

Everything matters:
- the mood of the horse
- the weather
- the horses around you
- the regularity of the exercise the horse gets
- the type of feed
- the riding environment

But there is more!

Aside from the environmental factors, riding is an especially difficult sport because of the balancing requirements inherent to moving through space on a living, breathing animal.

Obviously, there have been thousands upon thousands of "mutually beneficial" partnerships in the past and in the present; apparently, the human body can in fact become united with that of the 4-legged horse that travels so relatively effortlessly over the ground.

The trick is to learn how to become harmonious – how much to give, how much to take, and when to accept what is being offered to you.

So many questions!

You must learn to differentiate between too much, too little and just enough; between too early, too late and just in time; between resisting, energizing and being plainly passive. When is the horse going too quickly, too slowly, too enthusiastically, too lazily? What do you do in each case? How do you combine all your aids to communicate the right message at the right time? How do you not only refrain from interfering with your horse, but even learn to improve your horse to become better than his original state?

What is the answer?

There is no easy answer. The most obvious consideration is to seek out a credible instructor well versed in not only in all things 'horse', but also in instructional techniques and experience. There is no replacement for an 'eye on the ground' – no blog post, no (however well written) book, and no video – although such media do play a role in the over-all education of a rider. The person on the ground is the one who translates what the rider is doing now into what the rider can do in the future.

The other task, however difficult, is to try, try, try and try again. Pack it in one day, and start all over again tomorrow. Learning to change muscle memory and developing a blueprint takes time, dedication and repetition. Each time you change the 'rules' on your horse, be ready for a step backward before a new step can be reached. There is no other way.

Be patient – with yourself and your horse, and find joy in the pure accomplishment of learning from your horse; focus more on the journey rather than the goal.

17 The Top Eight Biggest Riding Mistakes

Making mistakes isn't always a bad thing. It's quite natural to make mistakes while we learn new skills, and often, they send us onto more appropriate paths. However, in horseback riding, there are mistakes and then... there are M*istakes*.

The kind of Mistakes that end up causing more pain than gain.

The reinventing-the-wheel ones that you don't actually have to go through personally to learn from. The Mistakes that you'd rather not go through – but unfortunately, many people do.

Here are the top 8 mistakes to avoid while learning to ride.

8. Taking your ego into the ring.

One of the first things you'll learn from horses is how to be humble. Whether you ride in a lesson, on the trails or at a show, do yourself and your horse a favor, and park your ego at the gate. Go to the ride with a positive, willing attitude. Appreciate your horse, your instructor and the other people around you. Appreciate *yourself*, what you can do that day, and how you are developing your skills over time.

And remember that each day is but a snapshot of progression in your overall riding career. Even if you feel like you might be going through a set-back, do what you can during that ride, give your horse a well-earned rest, and come at it again another day. You might be surprised at how you and your horse progress if you can let things go at the most critical times.

7. Not setting goals.

You can't just do the same thing day after day and expect progress. When you set goals, make sure they are broken down enough that they are realistic and achievable for both you and your horse.

You and your horse are a team, and as such, your goals should reflect both your needs. Plan to develop your biggest "need of the moment" – whether that need is yours or your horse's. Follow a systematic approach to skill development and work on small steps each day.

6. Trying too hard.

There is such a thing in horseback riding. If you get wound up enough, you can fall into a do-it-until-you-get-it trap. Horses often get caught up in this problem too, because their riders just don't know when to quit.

It's one thing to try, try again. But it's another to mindlessly keep repeat the same thing when nothing seems to be going the way you want it to. If, after you give it your best shot, you are not seeing the results you want – take it easy and come back to it another time.

5. Being closed minded.

Although there are three official Olympic equestrian disciplines (jumping, eventing and dressage), you can trot over to your local agricultural society to see how many different riding styles there are in just your community! Add to that the plethora of horse-related activities around the world, and you'd be hard-pressed to list them all on one page.

Each of those disciplines have their own way of teaching, learning, training and performing. While it's true that the horse is the common denominator in all of them, you'll find many cross-discipline takeaways that might address your needs in your particular riding style.

Stay open minded and be willing to "listen" to others, regardless of their riding styles.

4. Listening to everyone.

The other extreme though, is to listen to everyone. If you've already done something like this, you know how easy it is to get lost in the shuffle of opinions, especially when you are first finding your way in the equine industry. You might find completely opposite methods and recommendations for the same problem! What to do?

Once you have found your riding niche, seek out a reputable instructor or mentor and stay with that person for some time. Learn one system well. Move on only when that system doesn't meet your goals. Otherwise, give it a good effort and stay the course.

3. Riding horses that are too difficult.

This invariably happens to many of us at one time or another. Horses have different personalities, and some can be more challenging to ride than others. Honestly assess your skill level when deciding on a horse to lease or buy.

Get a horse that is more trained than you are if you are a beginner rider. Only consider less trained or younger horses if you have an accessible professional available to you, or if you have already apprenticed under a more advanced rider or instructor.

It won't do you or the horse any good if you feel intimidated by the horse. Many terrible accidents happen when there is a mis-match of the horse and rider's ability levels.

2. Not taking lessons.

I've spoken about this many times. There is no replacement for lessons. Even the best of riders need "eyes on the ground" to give them straightforward feedback. What you feel and what is really going on don't always match, and getting professional guidance in the quickest way to improve – for your horse's sake!

1. Being afraid to make mistakes.

Has this ever happened to you? Everything seemed to be just great until your instructor asked you to do something new. In one short lesson, you went from being on top of it all to feeling like you've lost everything you've worked so hard for.

The trouble is that while we strive for perfection, we might avoid trying new and different things that can help us find new skills. Sometimes, trying something new feels more like a set-back than progress. Maybe you lose some aspect of your position or your aids. Maybe your horse feels stiffer or more braced through the back.

If you feel like everything you've worked for just fell apart, don't despair! Struggling through a learning curve is only bad if you let it bring you down regularly and riding poorly becomes a habit. If you are going through a learning phase, though, it might be just what you need to do before you can put it all back together – better!

18 Fourteen Ways to Have A Great Ride

Summer time is when riding season moves into full swing. The horses are fit and the riders are well into a routine, achieving personal goals and heading out on trails. Here are some quick ideas to add to your normal repertoire of horsin' around activities.

1. Enjoy a good groom before you ride. Find your horse's itchy spot and scratch it! You'll both feel better after a thorough clean up and check.

2. Change things up. A switch-up can be just the change you need! Take a lesson, ride the trails, go to a clinic. Do something you don't normally do and enjoy the fresh perspective you get from it.

3. Play with transitions. Don't force them, but put in more than you usually do.

4. Build up energy. Don't get humdrum about your ride – go to it like it's the best part of your day (it is)! Think impulsion and engagement – from both you and your horse.

5. Ride with friends. Your horse likes it as much as you do – just limit "hanging out" and socializing until after the ride. While you're on your horse's back, ride with a purpose – together.

6. Do something new. Set up a new obstacle or jump. Or ride around the clump of grass. Here's one: weave through two barrels (or pylons or jump standards) – backward! Look for something different to do.

7. Set a goal. Work toward something that is achievable and sets you up for success. Transitions, anyone?. But do more than just that (see #5).

8. Let your horse take initiative. Encourage your horse when he does something well, even if you weren't asking for it. For example, if you asked for increased energy at the trot and he did a wonderfully balanced canter transition, go with him for a few strides. You can always go back to the trot again and continue to work on the energy level.

9. Have a quick celebration! Every horse has a favorite movement. After a series of "work" movements, have some fun time. My horse LOVES to lengthen or stretch – I use them as mini-riding-parties every ride.

10. Give your horse a pat. With your inside hand, so you can give an inside rein release at the same time.

11. Work on your half-halt. Find your horse's happy place with effective, well-timed half-halts. Balance is where it's at – for both you and your horse!

12. Keep you and your horse straight – even on a circle! Straightness is key to help your horse carry you around with as little damage to his body as possible. Constantly work on keeping the horse "between the legs and reins".

13. Go splash in a puddle. Literally! Use every puddle as an opportunity.

14. Hose your horse off at the end, especially if it's hot outside. There is nothing nicer for a horse than a cool (or lukewarm) shower after exercise. Washing the sweat and grime out from under the coat is a great way to end a great ride!

19 Finding Your Comfortable Un-comfort in Riding

She let out a tiny squeal and from the ear-to-ear grin on her face, we knew she had finally figured out what she had to do to get her horse moving forward.

"He feels like he's floating!" she announced gleefully. We knew that was horse-speak for the feeling we all get when something goes right and we experience a new "feel". It is the kind of feeling that we are always aiming for but rarely seem to find.

We celebrated with her, knowing how difficult it can be to coordinate all your body parts to get it right that first time. She was still giggling with glee although her horse had already slowed to a stop, sensing that she couldn't keep all her aids active for much longer than a few strides.

But that first time was all she needed to go at it again.

Many of us can relate to the scene above. Have you ever been in that position – the one when you finally discovered what it was that you were doing (or *weren't* doing) that pushed you just over the edge and gave you the breakthrough you were looking for?

Riding can be like that.

You can never become too complacent because if you are not the one spurring (pun!) yourself to newer heights, invariably, your horse will help you along!

Sometimes, people get comfortable enough to forget that they need to keep learning. At times, we might fall into the trap of believing that we are done with learning in riding. But the truth is that the learning never stops. There is always something more, a different angle, a deeper feeling. We can't become complacent in the training process of riding – we must ever strive for more, reach higher, try something new.

We must find the un-comfort in our comfort zone.

In yoga, it's called "changing your edge". First, you find the spot that starts to challenge you. Then you back off 5 percent. In this manner, you progressively reach higher while still working within your limits. You continually push yourself out of your comfort zone, but only just enough to make a small improvement.

Set your goals so that you are just *that* little bit uncomfortable. If you stay in your comfort zone, you will always ride the same way. The same successes will arrive at your door and the same problems will continue to haunt you forever more. Even if you change horses, the same problems will rear their ugly faces again and again, for it isn't the horse that has the difficulty, but you as the rider.

It behooves us to become better riders, on a continual progressive scale that dares us to progress beyond our current means. Although goal setting is a step in that direction, the objectives themselves can get lost during the riding session if something else pops up that attracts our attention. So it is with careful reflection that you must decide during the ride how to find that small un-comfort that will drive you to improve the horse you have that day.

Try to let go of your idea of success. Instead, focus on the process of the change you are putting into place. Instead of looking for the result, work on the movement step-by-step, and see how the result turns out. If it is not as good as you expected, don't worry. Just try again. You know then that you are still in your un-comfort zone.

If, on the other hand, the result is satisfying, then you know it's time to find the new edge. Once again, identify your (new) comfort zone, then extend it that much further. Then back off 5%. See if the horse can meet your expectations at that new "edge".

And so it goes – new goals, new un-comfort zones, new accomplishments.

20 Ready? Steady! (Or How To Ride Calmly And With Consistency)

Achieving consistency in riding is not a matter of waving a wand and then simply hanging on for the ride. It's more than learning a few "tricks" and hoping they all fall together in effortless synchronization. In fact, riding smoothly through transitions left and right, up and down while maintaining a steady rhythm and impulsion, outline and self-carriage is nothing to be scoffed at!

If you have tried to put together a series of movements, you are probably familiar with how you need to be aware of the horse's balance. You likely know that you need to actively maintain the horse's engagement through the various bends and figures in order to maintain a rhythmical, uniform look and feel to your ride. You understand that in horseback riding, in particular, a *lack* of excitement is a highly desired state.

You see, it's because what we interpret as calm or routine might be just the right thing for horses and their riders.

The opposite – confusion, frenzy, turmoil – all paint a picture (and feeling) of discomfort and disarray. In riding, excitement manifests in ways that indicate discomfort for the horse. When a horse bucks, rushes or pins his ears, he is sending out messages that he is not feeling good in his work. The rider that has to make a spectacle of riding by using loud or overly active aids or voice cues certainly gives the spectator something to look at, but is inevitably not riding for the benefit of the horse.

What It Takes to Be Steady When You Ride

Boring is very underrated, but highly valuable in horseback riding. You might be tempted to think that you are watching paint dry when you see a horse flowing effortlessly from one figure to the next, setting a consistent rhythm regardless of what he is doing, and a rider that is just "sitting there". People might complain that riding (especially flat work) is not a spectator sport and therefore not deserving of attention.

The truth is that both the horse and the rider have to achieve a very high level of proficiency to portray such composure and tranquility. To appear to be doing nothing, the rider and horse must both make continual adjustments to their balance, in order to stay in balance while they progress in space, together, through various movements. How do they do it? Here are a few ideas.

1. Maintain energy level

Impulsion is the first main component of any riding. Keeping the energy at a steady level requires a horse and rider that are adaptable and quick to respond to changes of balance. Too much energy, and the horse falls to the forehand. Too little energy, and the hind end disengages and the horse again falls to the forehand.

You need to ride strategically in order to keep the energy at the most effective level that helps the horse maintain a comfortable balance. Use half-halts to prevent the horse from running out from underneath you. If you can aid quickly enough, and your horse is responsive enough, you will be able to control the leg speed but allow the energy to be transferred over the horse's topline. You can develop a rounder, bouncier gait by half-halting so the energy doesn't just translate into leg speed.

On the other hand, you may need to use leg aids to help the horse increase his energy level when coming to a more difficult movement. For example, horses tend to often "suck back" when coming into a corner or turn. They might shorten their hind leg stride length and hollow the back, resulting into a bracing movement through the corner.

To counteract the drop in energy, use both legs to urge engagement of both hind legs. Maintain the rhythm that has already been established by *not* allowing the horse's legs to slow down in the approach to the corner.

2. Maintain straightness

The moment the horse loses straightness, the rhythm and energy level is affected negatively. The straighter you can keep your horse, the easier it will be to establish energy and impulsion. So in a way, impulsion and straightness are interchangeable much like the chicken and the egg – which one is needed first to improve the other?

You must know your horse to answer that question. Some horses lose straightness because they lack impulsion. So the secret to helping those horses move straighter is to get them to work better from the hind end. Other horses lose impulsion because they over-bend in one direction, or brace into stiffness in the other.

These horses have plenty of leg movement, but they drift out or fall in, perhaps because they have too much energy that is ending up on the front legs. These horses would need half-halts and secure aids that encourage them to keep their body in alignment while they move.

Straightness isn't something that anyone is born with. Both the horse and the rider likely have a stronger and weaker side and the resulting movement is determined by how the rider can control both her and her horse's crookedness. This takes time (years?) to develop but yes, you can chip away at it slowly but surely and one day. realize that your horse is tracking straight on the lines and bends.

3. Communicate

Constant communication is one of the key ways to maintain consistency. Through half-halts before and after each maneuver, the horse/rider team shares in the knowledge of things to come.

Use leg and rein aids for bend, turns and to reinforce half-halts.

Use your voice to reinforce your aids, and always be sure to acknowledge your horse's efforts while you ride. The quiet rider is the one who is communicating subtly but regularly enough to avoid any surprises.

The confident horse is the one who indicates that he knows his job and what is expected. You will know that you're on the right track when someone says that it looks like you're doing nothing, while the horse is floating along with an active regularity seemingly under his own initiative.

4. Practice

Well, it is true that (as close to perfect as possible) practice makes perfect. There is no replacement for practice, and all you have to do is get out there and put the time in. Well, maybe it isn't quite that easy.

You have to put in the best quality rides in that you can, over time. Maybe that means that you need more than one lesson a week with a qualified instructor. Or maybe it means that you and your friend can help each other out by being an "eye on the ground" and giving each other feedback. However you want to approach the concept of "effective" practice, make sure that you develop a routine for the benefit of both your body and your horse.

Here is your "homework":

Think about your rides and how you might be able to develop more regularity and steadiness in what you do. Even if you don't maintain "perfect" rhythm and stride length through your whole ride, see if you can be steady for longer and longer periods of time.

As you and your horse get better at maintaining rhythm, energy and stride length, make things more challenging by introducing more transitions and changes of bend. Work on developing flow, swing, bounciness, roundness, and all those things that make your horse snort and release through the body   even   more.

21 Why Rising Trot Is Not Rising At All

Not all rising trots are equal.

There are three reasons we rise at the trot. First, we might want to take our weight off the horse's back – and the easiest way to do it is to rise (or "post") every other stride in rhythm with the horse's movement.

Second, maybe we want the horse to have the opportunity to reach further underneath his body with his hind leg. By rising while the outside shoulder reaches forward (called rising on the "correct diagonal" leg), we remove our weight from the saddle just as the horse's inside leg comes off the ground. This encourages and allows the horse to step deeper with the inside hind leg, which is the balancing leg especially on a turn.

Third, we can influence the horse's activity level – we can change the horse's leg speed by posting faster or slower. The horse tends to follow the tempo of our seat, and if we can control that tempo, we can be more effective without ever having to go to the hands or legs.

The next time you go to a show, or visit the barn when there is a riding lesson, stop and analyze the way that the riders ride the horse's trot.

Look for the riders that appear to be working most in tandem with the horse and then watch their technique. What do you notice?

They don't move up and down.

Instead, they move *forward and back* within the movement of the horse. That is, their pelvis comes forward to the top of the pommel, hovers there for a moment (or even two), and then gently settles back into the saddle, *off* the cantle (ideally).

KATHY FARROKHZAD

The "forward" movement follows an upward arc toward the pommel, and the "back" follows a similar arc. The knees are soft and the angles demonstrate little change.

What they are not doing is standing up and down in the saddle.
There is very little rise. Why not?

When you move straight up and down, you fall behind the horse's movement. As you work to regain your lost balance, you come back down heavily and push your weight straight down to the ground. This might shorten the horse's stride, throw him off balance by putting him to the forehand, and may even cause back discomfort over the long term.

Stay in balance in the trot.
If you can move forward and back with the horse's movement, you can maintain a much more organic balance. Use the trot bounce to send your pelvis on the arc toward the top of the pommel and steady yourself at the top of the movement with your inner thighs. Then arc back with control so you can mindfully rest on the horse, causing as little discomfort and interference as possible.

If you can move efficiently within the horse's movement, you can even influence the horse's length of stride and speed. You can slow down the horse by slowing your posting down, or conversely, you can speed him up.

The next time you ride, pay close attention to your rising trot technique and play with forward/back versus up/down.

86

22 Why a Release is Not a Let Go

Release your seat after the half-halt. Release your legs when the horse moves away from pressure. Release your aids to reward the horse. Release the inside rein to allow the horse to bend deeper to the inside.

Sometimes, we use the word "give" in place of release. Please use it interchangeably here.

In horseback riding, we can release any aid at any time: the reins, the seat, the legs. Regardless of riding discipline, we have to release our horses for hundreds of reasons. We use that word so many times in so many ways. But do we know what it really means?

Many people interpret the term literally as it sounds like it should be – a freedom, a giving away or a letting go of the aids. But in riding, a true release is (unfortunately) much more difficult to accomplish than simply dropping everything!

Let's change topics for just one minute to illustrate the point.

Do you watch any of the world figure skating championship? As I admire the exquisite coordination of the pairs and dance skaters, I am reminded of the level of harmony we need to produce with our horses to show a similar fluidity of movement. Of course, anything I watch becomes somehow related to horseback riding.

So here is the scene: the guy lifts the girl, they do an intricate twist and thingy in the air, and then he "releases" her back to the ice. When you watch them, you see how carefully he carries her back down. What he *doesn't* do is drop her – or, simply let go.

The horse has four legs and he won't fall when you let go. It is true. We see riders "let go" of their horses all the time, and rarely do the horses fall to the ground (although some might stumble or trip).

Thankfully, the horses hold their own and make up for the rider's lack of timing or aids or knowledge. But what does suffer is the horse's (and by extension, the rider's) balance. Some horses lose confidence in their riders. Others learn to tune their riders out and just truck along on their own. Many plod along on their forehand year after year, doomed to some sort of lameness due to incorrect movement.

In any case, communication suffers, sometimes without the rider even knowing it.

What to do?

What *not* to do: let go.

Don't let go of your reins. Don't let go of your seat. Don't take your legs off the horse. Don't flop in the saddle.

Instead, work on a gradual giveaway.

Slowly reduce the pressure.

Leave your legs on but become less active.

Hold your own body but go more with the horse.

Keep a soft, delicate finger contact on the reins so your horse knows you are still talking to him.

Under all circumstances, maintain your balance.

Look for any and all reasons to release your aids.

Don't we all wish we could ride in lightness and complete balance? Just be weary of stopping or giving away or letting go completely.

Try to ride with the horse and work towards harmony and connectedness. Listen carefully to discover when your horse needs your support and when you should allow him to find his own way. There is a happy medium somewhere in between let go and absolute control.

If you can find it, you may also find a happier, more confident horse!

23 Breaking The Cycle: It Might Not Be What You Did Do...

...but rather, what you didn't do.

Time and again, we find ourselves having the same problem with our horses. We have worked repeatedly on a particular skill only to be faced with the identical issue once more. We try to resolve the situation using tools we already know but to no avail; the same result is obtained, and it isn't the one we are looking for.

We blame ourselves.
We blame the horse.
We try harder.

We get emotional. Surely, the horse would do what you want if he wanted to please... right? Why is he not responding?

And then, we do it all over again. We use the same aids, go through the same exercises, approach the problem from the same angle(s).

Need a Change Up?

To modify the situation, we need to alter our perspective. The unfortunate part is that often, the change that is needed is not easily accessible or acquired. Sometimes, no matter how hard we try, we simply cannot adjust ourselves in the manner required by the horse, simply due to inexperience or lack of skill. But that does not alter the fact that the horse needs something we might not be able to give him.

The Essential Instructor

There are so many possible ways to approach a riding problem. Unless we have the opportunity to ride many horses under good instruction for many years, we may not be aware of the approach that is needed for the particular situation our horse is facing.

Finding an accurate solution may in fact be impossible for us to reach on your own, especially if the problem is something we have not experienced to date. Enter the essential instructor: there simply is no other way.

What our horse might need is a completely new perspective. Perhaps we have to learn something new that we would never be able to dream about without the help of an informed instructor.

Practice and Time

Don't kid yourself – new riding skills take time to develop.

The necessary change-up may require numerous repetitions until we become proficient and effective enough to be able to change our horse's performance. We need to be content knowing that we are on the right path and that walking the path may take longer than we originally anticipated.

Changing the Rules... Again

Finally, we need to recognize that in changing our own responses to the problem, we are also expecting the horse to change his behaviour. Not only will we need to master the new skill, but we also must de-program our horse's responses that we blueprinted into him, and replace them with new ones. Although we usually find horses to be extraordinarily forgiving and patient, it will nevertheless take time to explain the new rules clearly enough to make changes in his responses.

Listen to Horses

We will know our goals are being achieved by being sensitive to our horse's reactions. If we uncover more tension, insecurity, lameness, tail swishing and/or pinned ears, we know we are not quite on the path we are seeking. In contrast, if our horse gives us snorts, bolder, more confident forward strides, strength and roundness and/or soft expressive eyes and ears, we know we are on the right track.

So the next time you get stuck in a rut and don't know what to do, think of what you *didn't* do, and give that a try!

24 Seven Reasons Why "It Depends" Is the Right Answer

It seems like everywhere you turn, someone has a different opinion about what you should do when you ride.

There might even be the time when the *same* person tells you to do two completely opposite things during one situation.

Let's take your coach for instance. One day, she says you need more leg to get the horse going better. Another day she says to half-halt more often and slow the legs down. Bend more here, straighten up there.

Make up your mind already! How is it that so many variations apply to the same outcome?

Obviously, the last thing we want to know is that there are seemingly endless variations to a multitude of skills that we have to learn if we want to be effective riders for our horses.

But when it comes to horses, the only "truth" is that there are many truths. It is our calling as riders to figure out which one works when and why. The learning is never-ending and even when you think you know it all, another horse comes into your life to bring you back down to earth (hopefully not literally).

Here are 7 reasons why "it depends" might be exactly the right answer to your situation!

1. Your horse might be very accommodating.

When your horse works at his best, the sky is the limit! You can do almost anything you can think of – with very little effort coming from you! These moments teach you how much you can do and how the aids combine to make everything come together. Your aids can whisper and you can float along almost as if you aren't there. Your horse's responses might come easier, and he also appreciates the harmony.

2. Your horse might be excited.

An excited horse may need more guidance, simpler and quicker aids. The quiet suggestive aids from yesterday may not be adequate if the horse is distracted or unresponsive in some manner.

You might need to seek his attention and work harder to make more basic requests. You might not be able to do the intricate moves from yesterday simply because his frame of mind is different.

3. The weather conditions might be different from the day before.

Almost all horses are affected in some way by temperature or precipitation. Riding the same horse on a hot muggy day or in pouring rain or in freezing cold temperatures might require different strategies. Discovering your horse's preferred weather condition makes the ride easier but working in less than ideal conditions is also necessary if you want to stay on a regular program. You have to learn how to ride the horse during various conditions.

4. You might not be as coordinated as your last ride.

You might be the inconsistent one. Maybe you had a rough day at school or work and you come to the riding session tense and frustrated. Maybe you have a cold and your reactions are slow and laboring. If you can be sensitive to your own emotional and physical state, you can take steps to counter them once you get on your horse's back.

5. You might be trying something new.

Whenever we step out of our comfort zone, we step into insecurity and frustration. It is perfectly normal to go backward before you move beyond your current level of expertise. While you try to speed up/slow down/quieten the aids, you discover that you lose some of the mastery you once had.

The same happens with the horse if you are trying to teach him something new. Awareness of what needs to be done during the confused moments is the ticket to making it through the learning curve, both for yourself as well as your horse.

6. Your situation might be different from someone else's.

You go to a clinic and watch as someone learns or develops her skill during the ride. You come home and apply the same strategies and for whatever reason, things don't go the same way. In horseback riding, it is often unfair to compare yourself to others in the sense that everything impacts your and your horse's performance. By knowing the specific factors that go into your situation, you can make better gains.

7. Training level causes variations.

Both you and your horse's background and skill impact the next steps you can take. More often than not, you will discover that you have to go back to the basics and develop them before you can go ahead with higher expectations. There is nothing wrong with identifying a missing building block and working on that before you try to do something more difficult. Learning things step by step is a valuable and safe approach to riding.

I hear people's frustration when they ask a question and the answer isn't black and white or easily predictable.

But understanding the variables in riding is the key to knowing that it is perfectly fine to learn many strategies that will invariably end in the same goal. And when someone asks, "What do I have to do when…?"

The answer might just be, "It depends!"

25 Two Steps to Facing Fear While Riding Horses

Note: Safety first! Always use any of these suggestions at your discretion. Always check to see if your horse is reacting to some discomfort or misunderstanding, especially if the behavior is unusual. There is no one-way-cures-all method to riding. Feel free to change anything to meet the needs of you and your horse.

When you start to ride horses, there comes a time when you must face your own mortality.

Because riding horses isn't just about feel-goods and swoon-moments and lovey-dovey pet him behind the ears satisfactions (although those surely are wonderful occasions).

Invariably, one day, your horse looks you in the eye (or not) and says, "No!"

Or maybe it's more like he sees/hears/feels some great horse-eating monster-thing and suddenly, his flight or fight response kicks in and sure enough, he *flies!* Good luck to you, wingless human, who wishes to share in his space and time continuum!

After one or two (or more) parting of ways, you will surely begin to dread, or at the very least, physically tense, in anticipation of the next event. You might find yourself nervously looking around for the next monster. Occasionally, you might become reactive or even apprehensive and then you become part of the problem.

However, in possibly all horse disciplines, you are taught to never show your fear to the horse. If you do, the horse will pick up on your emotions and respond in kind. There is some truth to that. Horses are mirrors of us and often read our body language much earlier than we intend. So your tension can breed his tension and then you both end up spiraling into something that becomes much worse than it could have been.

Why Fear is Good

Never apologize for your fear. In horseback riding, think of fear as a good thing. It is what protects both you and your horse from danger and keeps you safe.

Fear can help you draw the line that guides you into making life-saving decisions. Instead of fighting it out with a 1000-pound animal, maybe it's ok for you to get off his back and call it a day.

Instead of pushing the situation to a level that makes you deal with something you cannot or should not or do not want to have to go through, you can tone down the exercise, going back to an emotional level that your horse can tolerate or that you can comfortably ride.

But sometimes, you don't get a choice in the matter. What to do then?

How to Ride Through It

1. Focus on Your Seat

Easier said than done, right? There is one key method to staying on when the horse throws you a spin, buck or lurch.

Loosen through your seat.

Take every bit of energy and strength you have, and through the up/down/sideways/lurch moment, *let loose*. Rather than tightening your lower back, make it move with the horse. Find that saddle and let your seat Velcro in and go in whichever way it has to. The rest of your body will follow (trust me on that!).

Put all your attention into (not tensing but) releasing. Stay open in your body. Avoid hunching over into a "fetal position."

Think, "Velcro seat!!"
Ride through it.
Keep your cool.
Stay consistent.
Don't get mad/even/offended or feel resentment.

Then, as soon as you have a semblance of balance and you feel confident enough to start talking (physically) with your horse again, go right back to what you were doing before the excitement began.

Do Step #2.

2. Stay on topic

Your job, other than staying on, is to be an *active* rider by continuing to give The. Same. Message.

Just like that. Calm, cool, and thinking… "We were having a nice conversation before you interrupted!"

Go right back to getting that inside bend. Restore your balance by re-establishing the horse's balance, rhythm, straightness, stride length – anything and everything that will help him go back to his calm outline and way of going.

Then be ready for the next time. Of course you're going to look for the next spooky corner. Or listen for the next sound.

It's perfectly fine and even useful for you to be aware of your surroundings. You *should* know what causes your horse's behavior and be able to predict what's coming next. Just don't let your horse do the looking.

Make sure that your body "stays on topic." You might not be able to stop the next spook from coming, but if you were planning on going with a nice bend through that corner, you aids should clearly keep telling the horse to bend. Sticking to the program helps the horse know that you are predictable and consistent.

Prove Your Leadership

The horse is almost always relieved to find that you are willing to be the leader in your horse/human herd. He will often relax and become more confident when he knows that despite the monsters that are lurking in every corner, he can boldly go forward and strong because you will guide his way. You will tell him what to do.

You will keep him safe, not (only) because you love him and have the best at heart for him, but because you can physically stay with him, and then correct or help him in his time of need.

Over time, you will realize that your actions will help your horse in his reactions. Your emotions will be more easily controlled and your confidence will allow you to stay purposeful, rational and active during the unplanned moments of your ride. Although there is always the potential for the unexpected, you can take steps to minimize the risks.

26 Five Ways to "Relax" While Riding a Horse

On the ground or in the saddle, the one thing that we *can't* do around horses is relax. They often say that some of the worst horse-related accidents happen when the horse has been standing around quietly and people have let down their guard, not expecting anything to happen. That's because just by virtue of their sheer size, horses can hurt us in one unfortunate moment.

The same goes for when we're in the saddle. Too much relaxation can make you into a blob of a rider, or prevent you from being athletic and aware enough to ride through a sticky situation.

So what's the alternative?

Here are some suggestions. Every time someone tells you to relax, replace the word (and concept) with some of the tips below.

Release or loosen.

I think the words "release" or "loosen" are much more accurate in terms of what we should be doing while we are on the horse's back. Focus on one area of your body (say your elbows, lower back or knees) and try to release the joints.

You might not even have to release or loosen all the time – just in short durations that last as long as your horse's strides. Find your horse's rhythm, and loosen in sync with the rhythm.

This allows you to support your weight and balance, keep your contact without fully letting go, but still find moments when you can allow the horse's energy through your joints and body.

If you can loosen after being tight for some time, you might feel a dramatic softening of your horse's tension, or maybe a surge of energy forward. Often, the horse will sigh or snort or just look more content.

Tone.

Remember that little kid that could make herself feel almost weightless when you went to pick her up? Maybe you were one of those kids when you were younger. Those children can make themselves light as a feather by tightening their bodies and wrapping their arms and legs around you once they're "on board".

You can probably carry those children for a long time without feeling tired – because they are doing half the work for you.

Try doing that while you are riding your horse. One of the ways you can look like you are relaxing on your horse is to *not* be a blob. In other words, hold yourself up. Be tall, be strong through your core, don't slouch and avoid falling to every imbalance.

Trust me, for those of us who are not used to holding our bodies in a toned manner, it might be difficult at first. But give it a try. See what your horse thinks of it. If you do it long enough, it becomes easier. And maybe, your on-the-horse toning might become more of a habit even when you're off the horse.

Harmonize with the horse.

One of the key methods to relaxing on the horse is to harmonize. If you can ride in better coordination with the horse's movement, everything becomes easier for both you and the horse. Nothing makes you appear to be more "relaxed" than being in sync with your horse to the point that an onlooker cannot tell where the aids come from.

Feel for your horse's footfalls. Time your aids according to the horse's strides. Find the best rhythm for your particular horse. And do your best to move with*in* the horse's movement.

Breathe.
And I don't mean big long yoga breaths while you meditate on your deepest secrets and passions! No, this type of breathing is much more practical. Make sure you are taking in a breath and releasing a breath *in rhythm* with your horse's movement. This is the kind of breathing that keeps circulating oxygen to your muscles and brain, so you can think and stay in balance!

If you find yourself huffing and puffing after a few minutes of trotting or cantering, chances are that you aren't breathing "enough" for the energy output you are producing. This usually happens when you are focusing on one aspect of riding so you forget to breathe.

Until your body can automatically breathe regularly while you get down to riding, you need to have a strategy that will teach your body how to breathe while you ride. I know it sounds silly, but try this. Think of a song that is easy for you to sing. I usually tell riders to sing Twinkle Twinkle Little Star -or pick a song that you know off by heart! But try it. You don't even have to sing exactly. Just say the words out loud enough that you are forced to breathe.

Do it while your horse is moving, and say the words in rhythm with the horse's movement. That's the key. Find your horse's rhythm, sing according to the gait, and keep riding. If you do this enough, your body will start to take over and breathe on its own.

Lengthen your leg.

Tension radiates through your body if your legs are tight. If you knee grip and contract through the thighs, your body automatically becomes less supple and more reactive to the horse's movements. I know how hard it is to loosen and lengthen the leg in movement. But it doesn't mean you can't try over and over again until it becomes more automatic in your muscle memory.

So there you have it. Looking relaxed on a horse can be a difficult and often lengthy process of developing your riding skills to the point of maintaining good basic equitation. The next time people tell you to relax while riding, tone your core, lengthen your leg, harmonize and breathe. They won't know any different!

27 Sixteen Tips For Safer Night Riding

There is something special about riding at night. Maybe it's the fact that your eyes can't take in nearly as much information as they can during daytime. You are left to experience your surroundings with other senses that you may normally filter out during the day.

If you ride in an area that is far away from city lights, you'll be surprised to notice how bright the stars and moon really can be.

The thousands of twinkling diamonds in the sky can make us feel like the tiny, insignificant creature that we are, and really bring home the awesomeness of endless space that surrounds us. But aside from the moonlight, most of your vision is reduced to distinguishing between blobs of grey, darker grey and black. It's quite hard to identify objects until you get a close-up view.

The nocturnal sounds are amplified – your horse's breath, his footsteps and the creaks from your tack.

The crickets and the frogs, the flutter of bat wings and the occasional rustling of undergrowth as a ground animals scurry about their business.

The most sensational part of nighttime riding is how it feels. The horse's gaits seem so much bigger, probably because you can't see how far each stride really goes. The breeze whisks past your cheeks in a way that makes you really feel each and every stride as you travel forward.

Night riding is a spectacular experience that appeals to many people, but there are certain precautions you should take if you want to embark on an adventure of your own. It isn't for everyone nor is it for every horse. Just one little problem can morph into a huge emergency. Here are some ideas to take with you if you choose to ride at night.

Ride when there is moonlight.

The moon really does light your path. No matter how small the moon on a given night, it can cast a soft glow over the area closest to you. It helps highlight the larger objects and can even outline a path or riding space for you.

If you ride during a full moon, you'll notice in amazement how it illuminates the earth and casts long shadows underneath trees and forested overgrowth.

You will really feel the darkness if you go out on a moonless or cloudy night. Although your horse can still see better than you can, no light makes it even more difficult to negotiate hidden turns or lumpy, bumpy paths.

Know the area.

I wouldn't go on a trail at night without having ridden it repeatedly in daylight. You need to know where the obstacles are, if there are any holes in the ground and where the critters might be active.

It is very easy to become disoriented in the dark. You must know which way is home, and where each path takes you.

Even if you are riding in an outdoor ring, it helps to know where the deep spots and bumps are, and where the fence line begins and ends.

Ride with a friend.

It's always advisable to ride in groups. Aside from the obvious safety factor, it's a lot of fun to share the experience. Your horse will also appreciate having an equine friend along.

Pick a suitable horse.

If your horse is the nervous type, night riding might not be something you want to do until you have excellent communication with your horse. There is nothing scarier than a horse spooking randomly in the dark, for both the rider and the horse.

If you want to try this for the first time, stay in an outdoor ring, close to the barn and enclosed by a fence. Then see how your horse handles the situation, and work on developing your communication so that you can feel safe during an unexpected event.

Beware of critters!

One time, I was riding at night in the outdoor ring. The horse pastures border the riding area, and there are trees that surround the open space further away. I was enjoying a wonderfully rhythmical canter when suddenly... there was scurry of brightness not too far on the other side of the fence.

My mare caught a glimpse of an undefined glow and stopped in her tracks, focusing on the object. It turned out that a small herd of deer were crossing through the pasture, bounding through the tall grass and shining their white fluffy tails in the moonlight.

My mare's high-headed snort interrupted their progress and they stopped still, noses in the air, trying to determine what on earth would be frolicking around in the riding ring in the dark!

Once they recognized the horse, they resumed their lofty bounce through the grass, deftly hopped over the fence and headed on their way into the forest. My mare watched them the whole way until they were long gone, but kept her cool.

We watched as they disappeared into the darkness and resumed our ride. But we did keep an eye and an ear out toward the grassy area they had come from!

Slow Down

Always err on the side of caution, and slow your horse down if something seems unsure. The horse's survival instincts will give you fleet feet even from a standstill, but it's always safer to stay at a walk, or go back to the walk, if you don't know what's in front of you.

Only trot or canter on a flat surface that you know is free from bumps and divots. Always return to the walk on unsure footing. Remember that the glories of night riding don't outweigh your safety. Think of your safety as well as your horse's. Done with due diligence, night riding can be a spectacular experience that memories are made of!

28 Six Things You'll Learn While Riding on the Trails

Kayla was all pumped up, bright eyed and bushy tailed (for real) as we flew on winged legs over the sandy terrain. The footing reverberated deeply with each footfall as I heard the soft, hollow-sounding thumps from each of her steps.

These were some of the best trails in the province! I couldn't believe that I was there, looking ahead but feeling the trees beside the trail fly by as my fearless steed kept up an eye-watering pace. Her attention was focused ahead to the horses in front but she was also keeping an ear back, listening to the rhythmical breaths of the horses behind.

There is nothing better than being involved in an activity you love, with an animal you love, with like-minded people all working toward the same goal. Although the above scene was a competitive trail ride, you don't have to ride competitively to get the same level of enjoyment and challenge. Just head for the trails, with friends or without, and explore the surrounding natural landscape at your preferred speed.

The trail provides opportunities that you just don't get in other riding venues. There are forested paths that weave through dense brush, or open fields covered in high, waving grass that surrounds your horse's legs. There are hills and bogs and cleared tracks and bumpy root-encrusted trails.

There are also fairly flat, fairly clear fields where you can enjoy practicing your riding skills without the constraints of walls or fences, in the open air where your horse is inspired to move more enthusiastically, covering ground with less inhibition or restriction.

It's not like riding on the trails means you won't learn anything. In fact, there are many things you can learn because of the trails, especially when travelling at trot or canter. Here are six.

Don't pull on the reins!

This is something that Kayla taught me really well, but is true for many horses. I know I've mentioned not pulling on the reins a lot, but it's mainly because I learned the hard way that grabbing the horse's mouth (or nose if you're using something bitless) only positions the horse to lean forward into the pressure, lean forward in balance, and move along at a faster rate – especially if you are at a canter!

Rather, use your seat and half-halts to balance the horse into a position that allows him to transition downwards. By all means, pull if it's your last resort, but don't be surprised if it doesn't bring the desired result.

It took a good amount of ring riding – and then, on the trails, where the environment can be significantly different - for me to really understand how to do a down transition from the seat and not the hands.

Feel the energy.

There is so much room for the horse to move in a more natural environment. So if you find your normally flattish, pluggish horse resembling a sprint runner (or doing a jiggy dance on the spot), see if you can "ride" that energy and put it to good use.

Feel the energy come over the horse's back and use it as an opportunity to memorize what it *really* feels like when the horse tucks under and engages. You can try to emulate that feeling later on when riding in the ring.

Slow down to turn.

If you drive a car, you know that you need to slow down a bit before the turn, take the turn, and then speed up again after the turn if needed. Same goes with the horse.

Although you might not need to physically slow the legs down, you do need to shift the horse's weight back before you head into the turn. Otherwise, gravity will work on your horse just as it does on a car – and you may discover that your horse has to scramble while careening around a turn.

So if you have a little speed going, check your balance before the turn.

Know when to trust your horse.

There is no better place to learn about your horse than on the trails. You really have a chance to bond and get to know each other, while also "becoming one" with nature. The more you ride on the trails, the better you'll know your horse's signs and signals – when he's on alert, when he's truly relaxed, when he's going to ignore your aids, and when he's honestly tired.

The more I rode the trails, the better I got to know Kayla's personality. I learned that she was super honest and rarely acted up unless there was a reason (stampede of cows coming straight for us). I learned that she would go go go until she could go no further – which meant that I needed to stop her long before she was completely spent. I also learned that I could ride a bold, fast moving horse with full confidence in her.

Bend your horse – for a reason.

Bend – it's often such a difficult concept, especially when riding in the ring. Try *not* bending when moving along a curvy trail, and you'll know why instructors harp on it so much. There is a reason that your horse should step under with the inside hind and "wrap his body around your inside leg": balance!

Be careful if you are approaching a curved path at speed because it's easy to lose balance if your horse is rigid or counter-bent. It helps if you can get him to look into the turn (flexion) and avoid leaning one way or the other. Getting a full body bend gives the horse the balance he needs and supples at the same time The trail is the best place to learn all about balance!

Smell the ~~roses~~ trees.

So far, I've talked mainly about riding the trails at trot or canter. That's probably because of my horse's competitive trail experience (you can't really take the speed out of the equation once she gets used to it).

But there is another huge facet to riding on the trails – the beauty. Our often hectic lifestyles tend to reduce opportunity to simply be in the moment and enjoy it for what it is.

Some horses love ambling along at a leisurely gait. Walking on the trails allows you to take in every aspect of nature – the smell, the breeze, the scenery, the squirrel scurrying off under the leaves…. We're heading into fall here in our neck o' the woods, and the brightly colored leaves and the swish of your horse's feet through the foliage is enough to make a good day great.

Happy trails!

29 Six Ways to Know Your Horse is Comfortable – While Riding

Your horse is healthy and sound. You've checked the saddle. The bit and bridle fit and your horse works well in them. You've got everything you need for your horse to be comfortable while you ride. Now the rest is up to you.

Is your horse really comfortable while you ride? If you listen carefully enough, he will tell you using his own form of communication. How can you tell? Here are six ways to gauge your horse's level of comfort – while you ride.

Snorts

This is number one. In the old days, my friends and I used to have "snorting" contests – as in, the first one to get the snorting horse was the winner. It was a fun way to really focus on our horses – and get them to work well and powerfully with looseness and comfort.

Check it out yourself. When you ride, pay close attention to when exactly your horse snorts. What is the circumstance?

Sometimes, it's because he did something (like canter on) that made him breathe deeper and have opportunity to move. Sometimes, it's after a correction – for example, fixing crookedness in the horse's body with your aids.

Horses always feel better when they move straight – and the snorts roll out right after it happens. In all cases, the snorts come with deeper breaths. There is something nice about breathing – both by you and your horse!

Slobber

There is a good kind of slobber that indicates a soft jaw, an active back, and this feeling of looseness in the body that indicates comfort and relaxation in the horse's body. It's not about the bit or the nose band – it's about how the horse feels inside. If your horse never develops a "white lipstick", there's a chance that he is tight-jawed or tense through the body. If he leans on the bit, or is resistant to your rein aids, you might need to look for ways to communicate other than just through the hands.

Use half-halts to keep your horse well balanced. Work towards using your seat more than your hands. Follow the horse's movement with your lower back when he offers impulsion. All of these skills help to develop a soft, well moving back that allows for better movement and ultimately, comfort.

Swing

A horse cannot swing if it is uncomfortable in his body (well, it is true that the best conformed horses have an easier time even when they are tense). But for most horses, tightness anywhere in the body will prevent the "bounce" – the movement feels flatter and the stride shorter. I think of it as a "cardboard back" – the rigidity resonates most in the back and I can feel the immobility and increased concussion through my seat.

I often write about an increase in "bounce" in the horse's way of going, but it's really more than that. Swing is a full-body movement, combining suspension, ground cover and looseness in the entire body. The back moves up and down in a clear, well maintained rhythm.

Floppy or "Light" Ears

You can tell a lot from looking at the ears. Perky ears are usually a sign that the horse is looking at something. Although looking around may be fine during most of your riding, the horse is externally focused. Pinned back ears are a clear sign of discomfort. Stiff, unmovable ears indicate tightness somewhere in the body.

The horse that is truly "in the zone" has different ears – they are soft and not directed at one particular focus point. The ears may flicker back and forth as they horse pays attention to you and what is around him, but they remain light and mobile. Even when the horse notices something around him, he only pays slight attention while he passes by the object.

Some horses can develop floppy ears. If you can ride your horse in comfort most of the time, you might be able to find those floppy ears! In general, horses that flop their ears in rhythm to their strides also demonstrate all the other signs discussed in this article. Full body comfort and release shows up in the ears.

Body Shape

They often say that the outside of the horse mirrors how the horse feels on the inside. So if you can encourage him to take a balanced, uphill, engaged outline, you can help him become more confident mentally as well. Conversely, the horse that moves with the hollowed back, moves in a crooked manner and carries his neck in an uncomfortable way will often be as tense and tight mentally.

The horse that moves with a round, swinging outline (that is not maintained through force but rather through tactful, educated aids) is the horse that feels good on the inside.

Confidence

In general, a happy, comfortable horse is also a confident horse. He is sure of his environment and of his rider. He moves boldly without a second thought. He has this "watch me" attitude that can't be missed. Confidence can be seen, but it can also be felt. If you are lucky enough to ride a confident horse, you might be bolstered by his attitude. Even as you guide him along the ride, he will help you achieve your highest goals.

It is possible to develop confidence in the horse. Over the years, through repetition and positive riding experiences, your horse may change little by little until one day, you realize that he takes things in stride (pun intended!) and seems to enjoy his accomplishments as much as you do. Let's face it. Pretty much anyone can tell a happy horse, even under saddle. He is the one that is bounding along, bright-eyed and bushy-tailed (yes, that's where the expressions come from), and just overall *looks* like he loves what he's doing.

And when that happens, you can't help but become infused with that same sense of enthusiasm.

Section 3: Life.

30 Four Mutual Grooming Strategies for Your Life

It's mutual grooming madness back at the ranch! Every morning, as soon as they are turned out, Roya and Cyrus take many moments not to munch on the freshly growing grass, but to say a good morning "Hi" through a wonderfully peaceful mutual grooming ritual. I imagine that they are celebrating the finally warm weather and blanket-less mornings in the summer sunshine.

After many minutes of massage, they finally wander off to graze the long growing grass in their pasture. While I watch them absorbed in their blissful morning, I think of all the different ways we could follow suit and metaphorically partake in mutual grooming through our own paths in life. Here are four ways we can mutual groom (without actually doing it)!

1. Pay It Forward
We often hear about paying it forward, and although it really is a cliché and maybe the fad of the day, the heart of the

saying is valid enough to be included in our mutual grooming session.

Because if, just for a moment, we could set aside our needs, desires and wills, and go ahead and do something nice/supportive/encouraging/ helpful for someone, without thinking about how it should or could affect us, the world would simply be a better place.

Next time you see an opportunity, do something kind for someone – not for any personal reward, but just because the moment arises and you can.

2. Helping In A Time of Need

We can't do everything all alone. Some things just need a friend (or two) to give us the boost we need.

Have you ever watched horses start their mutual grooming? One horse inches up a little at a time and takes a little fur-fluffing tooth-touch on the other horse's wither area. This is just the invitation – do you want to scratch my back if I scratch yours? Usually, the other horse enjoys the nibble so much that she starts edging her body sideways up to the first. One nibble becomes two and soon enough, they're both going at it in a sort of rhythmical exchange.

First one, then the other, back and forth. In the case of my two horses, this can go on for minutes on end. If one stops, the other starts up again!

Helping others is exactly the same process. First, you ask – are you willing to give me a hand? Hopefully, they reach out to you and give you the support you need. Then, you do the same for them when necessary. It's a win-win!

Collaboration is one of the most important social skills – not only for friendship but also for every avenue of life. Next time you notice someone needs help, don't walk away. Turn to her and offer a lending hand.

3. Including Others

In general, horses that mutual groom get along well with each other. They socialize with most members of the herd, but they tend to seek each other out when back scratching is in order. In a sense, they get a feeling of belonging in their own mini-herd.

We all have a need to feel included, especially when it comes to people we like or admire. In our hectic rush here-there-work- home-can't-pause-for-a-moment-to-catch-your-breath…stopping for a few minutes to include someone in a conversation can go a long way to making meaningful and lasting human connections. If you notice someone off on her own, invite her to join your group. Involve her in your activities. You'll be glad you did!

4. Lend a Listening Ear

I can watch horses mutual groom all day. Besides the soothing rhythm of their ministrations, I can see the interaction that goes on within the grooming. First, one horse nibbles, then the other. It goes on like a tooth-filled dance – first him, then her, then him, then her. They take turns. They contribute.

When your friend needs to say something, just stop. Look her in the eyes and give her your attention. Even just being there to lend a listening ear might make a huge difference in someone's life. If you can reach beyond listening and respond to her concerns, you can help her problem-solve through a troubled time, or give her some insight she might not have ever thought of.

When you think about it, mutual grooming can be interpreted as a significant act of generosity. If we would just take some notes from the Book of Equine, surely we could each make positive, lasting impact on other people's lives.

31 Ask 25 Horse People One Question…

…and get 25 answers!

This phenomenon is a well-known fact in the horse industry. Over the years, I've been approached time and again by people new to the horse world, in a mixed-up state of frustration and confusion.

Who do they listen to? How can *everyone* have a different way of doing something? Isn't there a 'standard' method in the industry?

New horse owners go to look for a boarding barn and discover that every barn has a different feed program, turnout routine, barn rules, and so much more. Or, they take lessons from one instructor and then watch a clinic and discover that there are many ways to train one movement. Turn the horses out 24/7 or leave them in most of the day? Ride with contact or go 'on the buckle'?

There are so many extremes to horse keeping and riding, and then there are all the gray areas in-between. Where is a newbie to start?

For example, look at the variety of disciplines found in the horse world. Although every horse has four legs, a head and a tail, you find such a huge variety of activities from riding (so many sub-classifications in just riding) to driving (almost as many possibilities as riding), vaulting, ski joring (look that one up), line/breeding classes, trick training, and so much more.

And you can't stop there. Feeding horses can be as varied and emotionally-laden as the discipline you choose. With the huge variety of 'complete feeds' as well as the old 'tried-and-true' grains, it can be hard to make a decision –

especially when even in one barn, there may be as many different types of feed as there are horses!

After you get past the information overload, you will realize that the various points-of-view are in fact, often helpful and inspiring. However, you may not agree with everything everyone says, and you may find that you are attracted to certain 'types' of horse keeping and riding over others. Part of the appeal of the horse world is that you can find your own niche among a variety of options that matches your wants and needs.

The trick is to find a mentor, or instructor, who is willing to take you under her wing for your first few years of horse ownership. You should find this person to be knowledgeable, competent, honest, and most of all, interested in seeing you progress into becoming a self-sufficient horse owner.

This person should be willing to explain his or her reasoning and teach you how to make an informed decision among the various options. She should be willing to listen to other opinions and then capably explain why she either accepts or rejects that opinion. Finally, your mentor should be interested in seeing you grow and meet your own goals.

Try to stay with that person for some time. Switching from coach to coach will only serve to confuse you and cause a disservice to your horse. Learn all you can before heading off to "greener pastures" because although it may be tempting to jump on the next (band)wagon, too many differing opinions too early in your understanding of the horse world will cause another well-known syndrome: "a little knowledge is a dangerous thing". Be sure that you stay with the person long enough to have a complete understanding, at least from their perspective.

There is another part that you must play too – you must read (books and magazines), watch videos, attend clinics and seminars, take courses, and find a good boarding barn and lesson situation that helps you acquire the knowledge you need to be a responsible, educated horse owner. In essence, you need to 'study'. No one else can do that for you.

And finally, we go back to the original question: what about the multitude of answers to that one (seemingly simple) question you asked? You have two points of reference to weigh the answer against. First, how does the answer balance with what you have learned to date (and ask your mentor for his or her opinion if you don't know). Second, just listen to your horse!

He will always be honest!

32 Thirteen Reasons Why You Should Be a Barn Brat

It's time we take back the term "barn brat"! This applies to you if you are 5 years old, or 50 (or more). If you are one of those people who spends hours at the barn, eagerly taking in all things horse, this one is for you.

Not only is time spent at the barn *well* spent, but here are 13 reasons why barn bratting is good for us – and more importantly – makes us better not only as equestrians, but as all-around humans.

Exercise

From grooming, to carrying feed bags, to walking between paddocks – you get a full body, cross-fit type of workout. It's completely organic.

You don't have to count reps or buy any equipment. All you have to do is get things done! And voila! Your body moves and you feel better.

Oxygen

Fresh air – the country type of air that invigorates and leaves you pleasantly drained at the end of the day. For those of us who sit still whether at school or work, the barn represents a chance to not only move but also to breathe. And if you get on the horse and go for a ride, you might be huffing and puffing in no time.

Natural Setting

Speaking of which – the natural beauty of most barn properties is another enriching aspect to our daily lives. Whether the barn is situated on rolling hills lined with oak board fencing, or forested trails beckoning exploration (or both), the barn provides us access to uneven ground, green grass, gorgeous trees and the smell of the great outdoors.

The barn gives us the opportunity to trade off concrete sidewalks and wall-to-wall houses even if for only a few brief hours.

Responsibility

One thing you learn at the barn is that you have to do what you have to do, especially if there is no one else around to do it for you. The horses rely on you for feed, water, turn out, turn in and even exercise. Their needs can't be shoved to the side of a desk even if you are sick or tired or if it's too cold outside. You get up and go no matter what because they rely on you. And that is all.

Social Skills

Barn brats tend to become socially adept even if they aren't naturally outgoing. When you spend time with fellow horse lovers, you can't help but to interact with the people who are there with you. The extra perk is that horse lovers come from all backgrounds, and in all sizes and ages. The barn is one of the few places that children can interact with adults on a mutually respectful and respected level.

Challenges

Things don't always go right/as planned/well at the barn. Sometimes, you have to go through a situation that you'd rather avoid altogether. But the one thing you learn is that you can face those difficult times and even overcome them when necessary. And that makes you a stronger person in the long run.

Be A Student

Hanging out at the barn sets you up to become a lifelong learner. Not only will you continually want to improve your riding skills, but you will likely appreciate how you can learn something from everyone.

Thanks to the horses' individual personalities and abilities, each horse will give you different experiences to learn from. Even if you don't take formal lessons, I would bet that you will learn new things on a regular basis just by being at the barn.

Being A Leader

Not only will you value being a learner, but you will also invariably become a leader in no time. Horses respond best to confidence.

Clear and effective communication skills will quickly develop to keep not only yourself safe, but also your horse.

Hang around regularly, and you might find yourself teaching others what you know.

Empathy for Animals

This is almost a given, but you'd be surprised at how much your natural abilities will be developed. You will be able to understand horse language, and interpret horse-to-horse communication. You might even become good enough to know what they say to you! More importantly, putting yourself into another's "hooves" will make you better able to do the same with fellow human beings in any life situation.

Team Work

Working together becomes a habit when you hang out at the barn. Even if you don't know the other person, you will find yourself gravitating toward helping each other, especially when it really matters. Four hands are better than two, two heads are better than one, and two people riding one horse is the best (one on the ground and one in the saddle)!

Riding Skills

Riding is a full-body, intricate workout that involves the coordination of the core and body parts you didn't even know existed until you sat on a horse. It does get easier over time, but this is one of those sports that has layers of learning and never-ending self-improvement. Just when you think you got it, the next needed skill surfaces and you're on a new learning path all over again.

Confidence

When you first hang out at the barn, your self-confidence might drop considerably until you know what to do and how things work. Certainly, the activities relating to horses and horse-keeping are sport-specific and not particularly common out in the "real world". Conversely, as you become adept at everything including riding, you become more confident not only at the barn, but also in your human interactions.

Real Life (vs Screen Life)

I saved this one for last because of its pervasiveness in our smart-phone society. Everywhere you look, you see people hunched over their phones with thumbs flying.

Except at the barn.

Granted, when we are standing around, we might check for texts and whatnot, but interacting with horses requires our full attention. The pure physicality of even walking beside a horse as you bring him in to the barn, and obviously when you ride, requires your absolute attention. Being around horses is the one place that keeps us living "in the present". There is no other way.

Well, as it turns out, barn bratting is not so bad, and maybe even better than you might think!

33 The Truth About Balance

One of the "golden rules" in riding is the seeking of the perfect balance. We all strive for balance – in our position, our seat, our movement with the horse. Another fundamental area of emphasis is in the horse's balance: too low, and the horse is on the forehand; too high, and we risk taking unplanned airs above the ground!

But there is so much more to balance.

The secret is identifying when you find the "perfect in-between" – and being able to replicate that just-right-balance regularly enough to reap the rewards. When considering horses, finding balance occurs in avenues other than just during the rides themselves. Too much of something can be just as harmful as too little, and the horse person must learn to 'listen' carefully to the horses to know how much of something is just enough.

You must find balance in:
– *hay*: too much is almost as bad as too little

-supplements: too much can be wasteful or damaging, and too little can be similarly wasteful and useless

-riding: too often, and the horse can get "sour"; too infrequent, and your horse becomes less fit, able, and mentally ready

-turnout: too long and your horse gets dirty/cold/tired/ "wild"; too short and your horse gets bored/sour/unhappy

-bathing: not often enough, and the coat gets grimy and bacteria can cause skin problems; too often, and the oil gets stripped from the hair and the coat loses its luster and shine.

Well, you get the idea.

There must be balance in pretty much everything, and all you need to find it is awareness and willingness to make the necessary changes to even out the scales. And whether you are sitting in balance on the horse, or achieving balanced nutritional requirements, you can be satisfied in knowing that the perfect-in-between is a great place to be!

34 Perfecting Perfection in Riding: A Lifelong Quest

Let's just face the facts – there *is* no such thing as perfection in riding!

It is simple and true: one merely keeps developing, and once a particular technique or skill has been mastered, the next (absolutely necessary) step must be reached for. It is inevitable – for the lifelong rider, there is no other way.

Often, the fact that perfection can never be attained *is* the reason we keep coming back for more. We discover growth in so many areas thanks to the interactions we have with the horse. If we can listen carefully enough, we will achieve goals that also transfer into other areas of our lives, making riding relevant not only to our physical development, but also to so much more.

We all have our flaws.

Some people are perpetual "hand riders". They ride more on the reins than with their seat and leg aids. Many people forever lean to one side, working against tightness or rigidity in their cores. Others have to struggle with a tight lower back and pelvis, always trying to release more than their bodies are willing to permit.

A few of us rush our horses and put them on the forehand, while others ride slow and flat so their horses are unable to use their hind ends and swing in their backs.

Finally, some of us eventually realize that we have *several* issues that must be overcome before we can reach our potentials as riders.

After a few years in the saddle, you will be able to identify your main weaknesses and strengths, and you will know what you need to work on for a very long time.

The same can be said about our horses.

Some horses are severely one-sided. Some horses have a behaviour they revert to as soon as something causes tension: rearing, bucking, ducking in or out, balking/quitting, etc. From an outside perspective, it seems obvious that everyone has something to work on at any one point in their development, and horses are not an exception.

So how does the concept of "perfection" fit into our many inadequacies?

We will never really find the perfect horse, nor will we ever be a perfect rider. However, it would be irresponsible of me to give you the impression that riders don't try to find perfection.

Of course we try for perfect.

We learn new skills, develop our weaknesses, practice over and again. Just when things seem to become insurmountable, and the same problems reappear repeatedly, we learn that it is essential for us to put the pieces together and invest the extra effort it takes to get over the hump.

We begin to revel in the moments of glory when they occur, and then continue doggedly when they disappear. We string together a series of great steps to make one movement shine.

Then we develop performance movement to movement. Here's how.

Six steps to perfection:

1. Take lessons.
2. Identify your "normal" (unconscious?) habits that might be interfering with the horse's movement, and work tirelessly on developing those physical skills.
3. Become an active rider and gently but firmly expect the horse to respond to your requests.
4. Watch better riders and analyze their reasons for success. Then try to duplicate.
5. Take more lessons.

6. Repeat!

35 Fourteen Reasons to Love Horseback Riding

Many horse riders will tell you about this feeling of "freedom" that you gain from the top of a horse's back. There must be hundreds of reasons why people enjoy horses and horseback riding. Here are a few experiences you will be privy to once you take a bite from that "apple" that is horse riding:

14. **Really, truly "interact" with the great outdoors.** Feel the air, smell the foliage, see nature's beauty, *and* get to travel through it all with your favourite four-legged friend.

13. **Develop your sense of body awareness.** Can you feel your arms/legs/core/*seat* in any other endeavour the way you can when you're on a horse's back? There is no other situation quite like being on a 1000-pound animal progressing through space and time, while you are considering what your

various appendages are doing. *Then* there is the rider's "seat" to keep in line…!

12. Become fitter and more athletic. It will happen organically and by necessity. There is no way around it – ride regularly, and you will find your body becoming more agile, able and yes, even fitter. Ride several times a week and discover all the glamorous physical by-products!

11. Discover "balance" in more ways than one. Of course your sense of balance will develop while you struggle with the power of gravity five feet above the ground. However, you will also discover the other balance truths – such as balance in feeding versus not (!), rest versus activity, shelter versus the great outdoors, and following versus resisting.

10. Develop new "nerve endings". Regular riding will begin to point out to you areas in your body that you might not have been particularly aware of before. Feel your fingers develop an alertness that will allow you to distinguish between "give" and "release" – even while you keep your fists closed.

Discover the nuances between lower legs that "wrap" around the horse versus the legs that grip and clench. Most incredibly, wait for the day that your seat can essentially communicate your very *thoughts* – with minimal use of the hands and legs – to your majestic beauty as he glides over the ground beneath you.

9. Be a witness to physical "power" like never before. The movement of a horse can at times be exhilarating, or at times downright nerve-wrecking, but the power cannot be contested!

8. Enjoy graceful connection with a horse. There is simply no other feeling like it. A horse is not the same as a dog, cat, or other domesticated animal. Try it one day – you'll understand what I mean.

7. Have something to talk about that most people don't relate to! Unfortunately, you will notice that most people in your life will "turn off" within the first five minutes of your description of that fantastic new feeling you discovered the other day while riding. Accept this as a normal side-effect and enjoy the few who relate to your descriptions even if they have never experienced it themselves.

6. **Find parts of your character that needed to be improved.** Invariably, you will discover characteristic traits in yourself that you never knew existed. Then, you will realize all the reasons why you must develop these qualities and continue your self-development toward becoming a better human being.

5. **Opportunities to go places you wouldn't go otherwise, and meet people you would never have met.** These days, horses and horseback riding can lead you far and wide and connect you to people from all over. Make new friends, travel to distant locations, and enjoy the most beautiful spaces on earth simply because you follow horses to new and unknown places.

4. **Make new friends who share your passion.** The love for horses spans across countries, personalities and cultures. Other people who are passionate about horses can be found almost anywhere you go – and the bond that connects is universal.

3. **Move your body in a way that promotes health and well-being.** From grooming and tacking, to walking around in the fields, to the physical movements your body "receives" while riding – these are all specific to the sport and otherwise not always accessible.

2. **Learn important life "truths" for your equine friend.** Listen to horses to find out all about relationships, leadership, social skills, communication. This list is endless

and if you can "hear" clearly enough, you will find many facts that transcend from the equine to the human.

1. Borrow a sense of freedom otherwise not available to mere humans. Many horse riders will tell you about this feeling of "freedom" that you gain from the top of a horse's back. Challenges, whether physical, mental, emotional or social are almost literally dropped to the ground the moment your seat is placed into the saddle that graces that horse's back. There is nothing else like it in this world.

36 On Enjoying the Path

I can hear you now – you're groaning… the path?? How can "the path" be fulfilling?

You might ask: doesn't "the path" translate to tedious repetitions, lack of acknowledgement or recognition, stumbling blocks, frustrations, steps backward more than forward, and all the other associated negativities that occur when something is practiced day-to-day, week-to-week?

What about the glory of the goal, the clear, final call of reaching the destination, the accolades and the photo finish? How about the sense of accomplishment, the personal gain, the reward of achievement?

Well, you're right of course. Goal setting is paramount in all activities, especially if they are long-term and difficult to complete. Without a sense of where we want to go, there would be no 'path' to speak of. And we all require and crave (at some level) for a sense of recognition and a feeling of a job well done.

But in horse riding, the majority of the time is spent on the path itself. The achievement of goals are short and fleeting, maybe because the horse is a living and breathing entity unto himself, and he has opinions, desires and interests that may not match yours! It is well known that there is a horse somewhere, sometime, that will humble every person. I would argue that the lessons learned from those horses might be the most meaningful of all.

Often, those lessons are not technical in nature. Rather, they teach us about our ability to persevere, to be patient, to set aside personal desires and ego, and so many other deep lessons that are essential in developing wholeness of being and strength of character. They develop our very human-ness and sense of place in the world.

And so, the next time you find yourself stuck on an exercise, struggling to achieve your next desire, and falling flat on your face (hopefully not literally) despite all your effort and dedication, try to step back and see the whole picture. What path are you on? Where have you been and where are you now? How does your current place in the (horse) world fit with where you want to be? What can you do to take just one tiny step closer to the end goal?

And remember, as E. Joseph Cossman put it so well, "The best bridge between despair and hope is a good night's sleep." Sleep on it, and go at it again the next day.

And enjoy the path!

37 How You Know You're at the Best Barn Ever

The quest for a barn that suits not only your needs but your horse's as well might seem to last a lifetime and propel you through many travels far and wide. Although it is sometimes difficult to find the first-rate location to plop down your tack trunk, don't despair! There are barns out there that do in fact meet all the following traits described below.

You'll know it when you find the right place. Like a pleasant afternoon sunshine-y day, the best-barn-ever leaves you feeling warm, content and satisfied – with your day, your ride, your horse and even with the wonderful interactions you had with like-minded people.

This article is dedicated to the barns that have mastered the difficult balancing act of meeting *everyone's* needs, horses and humans alike!

Here is how you will recognize the place.

1. The horses are roly-poly and content.

More importantly, they are healthy and vibrant. Their exercise program is conducive to maintaining good body condition and combined with a healthy and adequate feed program, the horses are able to work at their potential.

Their overall condition tells you the truth right away: the horses are receiving good care. Their coats glow in the sunshine and they have a bright, how's-it-going expression that welcomes visitors and barn staff alike.

2. The barn is gleaming.

A clean barn does more than just maintain good health for the horses. The spotless corners, clear aisle ways and web-free ceilings tell a tale of care and attention to detail. When everything has its place and everyone works at maintaining a clean and safe environment, there is a sense of calm that pervades over all the activities that transpire through the day.

3. Fellow boarders are friendly and helpful.

People are genuinely pleased to see you. They are happy to be at the barn and with their horses. They treat their horses like the pets they are while also committing the time and energy required to ride to their own high standards – not only for their own benefit, but especially for their horse's well-being. You can count on them to give you a hand in times of need and to cheer you on when you run into challenges.

Your success is their success and you are all on the same team. Somehow everyone knows that personal bests are the winning rides, regardless of the ribbon color. There is only one thing to beat and that is your past accomplishment.

4. You know you can count on a reliable routine and schedule in the barn.

The timetable of the barn is so well established that you can predict the routine to within a reasonable time frame. You know when supper is fed so that you can plan for a post-dinner ride. Lesson times are clearly written down for all to see and there is special attention given to ensuring free arena time each week for the boarders.

5. Special needs are discussed and accommodated as best as possible.

Just like people, horses can be quite different from each other. What works for one horse might not be beneficial at all for another, and the best-barn-ever manager has somehow managed to find a routine that accommodates every horse's requirements.

Individual feed programs are standard and supplements are fed regularly. The horse that needs extra feed will get what he needs. The horse that can live off "air" does not get overfed.

6. Quality lessons are available and everyone is interested in improving their skills.

It goes without saying that everyone benefits from the availability of riding lessons. Having a knowledgeable eye on the ground benefits the horse owner, the horse and the facility.

7. People are available to help the owner problem-solve through difficult situations.

One of the most difficult situations a horse owner undergoes is making complicated decisions for the health and well-being of her equine friend. There is nothing more uplifting and supportive than barn owners, managers, boarders and friends who listen, trouble-shoot, offer solutions and make recommendations.

Done in the right way, friendly support can go a long way toward softening the bumps and hurdles of the challenges that come along with learning to ride, owning horses and keeping horses healthy and sound over the long term.

8. Conflicts are addressed in a non-confrontational manner.

Conflicts happen everywhere and the barn is no exception. It is never the conflict that is the real problem – conflicts are a part of life and impossible to avoid.

Instead, the key is *how* conflicts are handled.

There is a wonderful synergy of intentions at the best-barn-ever. Instead of people looking to blame or criticize their fellow barn mates, they work hard to communicate, collaborate and concur with each other, solving problems together and contributing their particular talents for the greater good.

9. There are high behavior expectations.

One of the key factors in maintaining a comfortable and friendly environment is in the people themselves. The best-barn-ever has an environment that encourages respectful behavior not only for the animals but also for everyone else in the barn. Courtesy and politeness reign supreme and it goes without saying. People put regular effort into maintaining peaceful and polite interactions.

10. You think of the barn as your "happy place".

You are happy when you go there. Your horse thrives on his routines. The barn is a place where you can develop – physically, mentally, emotionally – to become the best person you can be.
The barn "just fits".

Before you laugh me off with ridicule, accusing me of fabricating far-fetched dreams that never materialize in the real world, let me assure you that I can think of several places that have mastered this art. Surely there are many barns that fit in a similar manner for each of us, wherever we may be in our horse listening path!

38 Ten Ways to Spot a Horse Person

Once upon a time, in a land not so far away, I was teaching in my classroom of little Junior Kindergarten children. I had a special event planned for them, and several parents joined us during the day to help out. You can imagine the fun we had – a room full of children, amazing treats and a bunch of put-a-smile-on-yer-face activities to keep us occupied.

You can probably also imagine the mess that was left behind as the lunch bell rang and all the little bodies headed straight out the door for recess.

Lucky for me, a few parents stayed back to help with the cleanup. One mother, in particular, grabbed the class broom and started sweeping. I stopped what I was doing and took a long look, admiring her sophisticated grasp of the broomstick and the refined dust-flicking movements that magically made the floor shiny and new.

She caught my gaze as I was analyzing her mad sweeping skillz, and looked at me with a puzzled expression.

"Where'd you learn to sweep like that?" I asked.

Sure enough, turned out she had horses. And a barn. And no barn help!

We had a chuckle that day about the funny idiosyncrasies of horse people, and how you can spot one from a mile away – if you know what to look for. Here are some clues, in no particular order.

1. Smell doesn't bother them.

Smell? What smell? In general, horse people have an easy time with the less appealing scents you might find around a barn or field – like the smell of rotting manure, dead rodents, or fermenting beet pulp. But don't be surprised if you catch them taking a deep whiff of air as they enter a clean barn, put their nose to a flake of fresh hay, or snuggle close to their horses.

2. They can clean up disgusting messes.

This goes along with the bad smells in the barn. After being in a barn for a while, they won't be nearly as disturbed by squishy, smooshy messes as the regular person. Clean out a few stalls, clear up a few corners in the barn and soon enough, there will be little that can turn them right off.

3. They have more empathy for all animals than the average person.

As keepers of a large animal species, horse lovers are known far and wide as guardians of those who can't speak for themselves. But for most of them, this love of animals transcends species.

They learn to appreciate all animals more, thanks to what they learn from their horses. Be it cats, dogs, lemurs, or goats, they'll be there to give a helping hand or just a cuddle.

4. They can stay out in all kinds of weather.

Whether in rain, drizzle, snow or fog, the horses are waiting for food and care. No excuse is good enough – someone has to get out there and do what needs to be done.

If the riders compete at horse shows, they'll soon become comfortable in all sorts of conditions – because the show must go on! Have no fear. They'll learn to dress adequately (not necessarily for fashion) and just go out and get the rides in, the tack cleaned and the horse gleaming. The job must get done!

5. They don't bat an eyelash when lifting heavy objects (say, around 40 pounds??).

I'm thinking about feed bags, hay bales, full wheelbarrows or awkward horse-size blankets. Horse people tend to do what needs to be done – sooner than later. If someone is around to help – all the better! Otherwise, roll up your sleeves and lift! Just bend your knees before picking it up.

6. They can drive a truck and trailer just as well as anyone.

And car. And bicycle. And four-wheeler. And anything else that moves.

Bonus! They can also drive them all in reverse!

7. They aren't shy to use the right names for all the "private" body parts!

Young children never learn to be shy about using the correct body part terms, because in a barn, no one gets too hung up over giggling over words. When the health of their horse is a concern, they make sure that they are perfectly clear about what body part they are referring to. Funky terms like *semen*, *sheath*, *vulva* and *teats* just become common vocabulary.

8. They have many and varied (non-school, non-work) friends.

The barn is a non-discriminatory venue. The aisles are graced with the pitter-patter of young feet, the creaky-patter of the more finely aged feet, and everything in between.

Various levels of ability become less critical when one is sitting on the back of a trusty steed.

When everyone has a common interest, it becomes easy to cross any gaps – social, physical, age, and more – and find things to talk about. It gets even better when one riding arena is populated at once by children, teenagers, adults and old-timers – all in it for one shared passion – the love of the horse.

9. They can push themselves out of their comfort zone.

Don't kid yourself. Riding isn't all fun and games. Learning to be around horses necessitates a level of confidence and carefulness that teaches horse people to accept the fact that things might not always work out. They will find themselves being humbled and challenged on a regular basis. Soon enough, they will recognize that stepping out of their comfort zone is valuable. That's where the real growth happens.

10. They STILL take a good long look at the horses in the fields as you drive by.

That little kid inside them who was mesmerized by horses never really goes away. They might mature and develop over the years, but one thing is for sure –

their attention will suddenly shift to wherever there is a horse to be seen!

39 Top 6 Reasons Why Horse Lovers Love the Earth

On Earth Day, as I think about the virtues of this planet, I begin to make profound connections between horses and the earth.

Caring for and riding horses must be among the most earth-dependent activities left to us (aside from farming and other such activities). Here are the top 6 reasons why horse lovers love the earth:

6. The beauty of mother nature that never ceases to amaze.

What is better than a scenic view with horses leisurely grazing in a luscious green pasture? Or how about the trail ride you went on that wove its way through paths, up and down hills into unknown territory?

From quiet sounds dampened with new white snow, to dripping icicles on a warming early spring day, to wildflowers blowing in a meadow breeze, to the scorching heat of the summer sun – each season brings its own marvels in the cyclical mystery that is life. There must be millions of memories etched in our minds of beautiful horse-related scenes that stimulate the senses and feed the soul.

5. The trees.

Trees are essential to the very basic needs of life; they provide shelter and purify the toxins we emit into the atmosphere. If you are lucky enough to have a (safe for horses) tree stand in your pasture, you know very well about the functional shelter they can provide from all the elements. They are also useful as snacks and back scratchers for some of our horses!

Trees are also master recyclers because of the very fact that they absorb the carbon in the air and release oxygen back into the atmosphere. We continue to have fresh air to breathe thanks to the trees that silently work their magic on the earth.

4. The crops.

One year, crops became a hot topic of discussion after a long, lingering drought that prevented the growth of most horse feed, including the basic staple of hay. Farmers were devastated by the lack of precipitation and although we were only somewhat affected locally, that small change in production was enough to highlight the importance of our farmers and food production networks.

Everything a horse eats can be traced right back to the earth – even the attractive designer bags filled with processed feed.

3. The air.

What we breathe provides us our very sustenance. Horses are as much affected by pollution as we are – maybe even more so. What we pump into the atmosphere stays in the atmosphere. While we expect our horses to perform athletically outdoors in the open air, we need to keep in mind our responsibility to reduce our carbon footprint as much as possible.

2. The ground.

The earth itself provides foundation for so many equestrian-related needs. You know what it feels like to ride in good footing. You also know how necessary the earth is when it acts as a base for a barn or an indoor arena. The type of footing affects moisture absorption, rendering a riding surface useless if conditions are not suitable – from frozen ground to muddy bogs, riding can be restricted or enhanced by the ground.

1. Raw materials.

Absolutely everything we have comes from the earth. This includes the metal that forms a horse's bit, the trailers that haul the horses and the gasoline that fuels our vehicles. Our homes and barns are made from materials that come from the earth. Our electricity, natural gas and running water originate in the earth.

There is simply no getting away from it. We owe our existence to the Earth. And our horses depend upon it.

40 Horseback Riding – the Yoga Way

When you are riding, do you "practice" your ride?

Do you give your horse and yourself a break when things go wrong? Do you approach "mistakes" with a forgiving attitude, thinking that this is just one practice in a million, and there will be chances to improve over time?

I have to admit to myself – not all the time. Sometimes, I get wrapped up in making it happen "right now". Sometimes, when things don't fall together at the right time, I feel discouraged. I feel like I've failed my horse. Other times, I feel like the horse has let me down.

Practice Your Ride

As I walked into the yoga studio the other day, I was greeted by my yoga teacher with:

"What a wonderful day to practice."

The word "practice" resonated in my mind for a moment. Naturally, I made a horse-riding connection.

"Practice" refers to repetitiveness, habitual performance and regular training. There is a sense of repeating to seek improvement. But the key underlying sense of the term is that if things don't go right, you can try, try again.

When you practice something, you know it doesn't count. The concept brings a positive sense to a situation. When you practice, it means you are trying to improve yourself. The world is on your side, you know you have a second and third chance. Mistakes are forgiven. There is room for improvement.

You have more time. You have more tries.

You can breathe a sigh of relief knowing that you'll be given another chance. You know that if things don't go as well as planned this time, you will eventually get to the point where you want to be, because you have all the time in the world to improve yourself.

Find the balance between achieving and letting go.

Of course we don't want to do badly when we ride. It is obvious that we want to seek harmony, stay in balance and be there for our horses. It is through practicing that we can discover the areas we need to improve upon and how to use our aids clearly.

But things do not always go as planned! When this happens to you, it is time to sit back and reflect – it's OK for things to not go perfectly. There is always the next try, the next day, the next week. Give yourself some slack. Be kind and appreciative to your horse even if you *didn't* get what you wanted right away.

Be prepared to try, try again. Maybe there is something you can change. Is there a different sequence of aids you can use? Were your aids too tight/loose/quick/slow? Is your horse in the right frame of mind? Maybe achieving only 50% of your goal is just fine for today. Discover the things not to do and as a by-product, the things *to* do. Keep trouble-shooting but avoid building tension and getting stressed. And if all else fails, quit while you're ahead.

Feel the freedom that practice can give you. It is not essential to be perfect, because so long as you keep practicing, the achievement will come on its own. Let it go and enjoy your ride!

There's always tomorrow.

I looked into my yoga instructor's eyes, enjoying the deeper understanding (and riding connections) I had just made with just that simple word "practice". I felt a sense of relief in knowing that I wasn't going to be expected to be *perfect* in my yoga practice that day. I also gave myself the permission to enjoy that same feeling in my future horseback rides!

Putting It All Together

Horses. Riding. Life.

Each one affects the other until they are all interwoven into one. For those of us who have chosen horses as our way of life, there is so much to be said about each and every experience we share with these magnificent creatures. I want to end this book with a short narrative about my first horse, Kayla Queen, who first took my hand (so to speak) and taught me the ways of the horse and the rich, fulfilling life that riding can offer. This is a "moment" inspired by the longest endurance ride of our competitive trail career, through some of the most beautiful trails in Ontario, Canada. Not only did I learn about horses and riding, but I also learned as much about life and myself. I hope you have as many opportunities to grow as I have had with my horses.

Were we going too fast? I saw the trail take a downhill slant and noticed a turn up ahead. The horse in front maintained his canter even has he negotiated the turn. I thought I was ready for it, and Kayla would surely slow down if she felt she needed to. We needed to keep up our speed in this endurance race but honestly, I was more interested in finishing than winning.

We had to simultaneously take the turn and balance through the downhill slant. Kayla went at it as if there was no change in the footing. But it had rained overnight and the slick ground underfoot gave way.

Before either Kayla or I could realize our error, all four feet swept out from underneath her, and we found ourselves skidding on a sideways slant, heading to the ground. Luckily, we landed onto a hill rising up to our right side, so the fall was short and soft. Kayla immediately found her feet and righted herself. I was on my side on the uphill slope, unhurt but quickly discovering that I was horseless.

Kayla looked for the horse ahead of us. The rider had unknowingly continued at the canter and disappeared from sight. I was on my feet but not fast enough to catch the mare. In a flash she disappeared around the turn in pursuit of the horse, and I was left to myself in a suddenly deafeningly quiet woods, with no assistance.

I walked around the corner, wild thoughts running through my mind. I started reviewing the event and all the "should-haves" popped into my mind. I should have slowed Kayla down – she was too inexperienced to handle that kind of footing at that speed. I should have leaned farther back as I noticed the downhill slant. I should have….

But I'm getting ahead of myself….

Very, very early that morning, we had set off on our adventure. The sky was still pitch black as we left camp, having waited for the most competitive horse and rider combinations to leave before heading out on the trail. In the dark, it was difficult to see the trail markers that were set up to keep us on track.

In the shine of the almost full moon, I looked down for guidance from below and followed the weaving path of crushed grass, already expertly drawn by the horses ahead of us. The tall autumn grass around us gleamed with wet dew and splattered cool droplets over Kayla's eager footfalls as we headed off on our second ever endurance ride, the 55-mile "Oktoberfest" contest.

It was early and it was cold, but this ride topped my horse riding bucket list. I loved my horse, and I loved riding the trails. The night before, I had enjoyed camping out with Kayla in her pen beside me, surrounded by a crowd of other like-minded horse lovers who were here for the same reasons.

The barbeque dinner, the night time bonfires and meeting people old and new was a joy in itself. The ride the next morning was the icing on the cake, a personal challenge that would help me determine if my conditioning program had been adequate, if our training was enough and if we had it in us to complete 55 miles of some of the best country in Ontario.

The night-like darkness seemed to last forever, and most of the beginning loop of the trail was completed before I could really see the surrounding scenery. At long last, the first hint of grey daylight began washing over the foliage around us, and I could begin to pick out the trail markers – ribbons of red for right, blue for left and white for straight.

I let Kayla settle into her own rhythm; being a Standardbred mare, her casual footfalls tended to be faster and more ground-covering than most horses. I had learned over the years to let her do her thing, as she had an uncanny way of picking through the terrain to find the best landing spot for each foot. She rarely got snagged in underbrush or took a misstep over tree roots or rocks. The remarkable thing was that she could do all of this – FAST!

I enjoyed the cool breeze as it swept over my face, thinking back to the "path" that had led us to this ride. Three years prior, I had been taking riding lessons at a local lesson facility when I saw Kayla for the first time. Impressed with her calm temperament and rideability, she was my "dream come true horse". I had spent my entire life to that point finding any avenue to be with, around or on horses. Kayla represented the end of "any" horse and the beginning of horse ownership.

She was a trained but never-made-it-to-the-track Standardbred mare. Having little experience with these horses, I searched for information and assistance in training a racing-bred horse. A little research revealed that Standardbreds had originally been raced at "trot under saddle" races in the 1600s in America. It was only about 150 years later that people began to race them in harness. This convinced me that her flair for the trails was more than just my own wishful thinking.

Typical to a retrained Standardbred, Kayla offered excessive speed at all gaits. She is a "free-legged" pacer. Even now, unridden, she often switches from the trot to the pace, a lateral gait where both legs on the same side progress together. When ridden under saddle, she was content to settle into a rhythmical, side-to-side sway that matched the speed of an average horse's canter.

Kayla's racing ancestry made her a prime candidate for long distance trail. Aside from her good "wind" (her large flared nostrils could exchange large amounts of air in each breath), she also had that can't-put-your-finger-on-it characteristic: heart. Having a strong intrinsic work ethic, she was most encouraged when she saw even the tiniest outline of horse and rider ahead. A competitive drive in a horse might be frowned upon in other riding disciplines, but in distance riding (and particularly endurance races), her insistence to always be first became a remarkable asset.

It took some time to learn how to correctly condition for a ride. At the time, I couldn't find other competitive trail riders in my area. I was left on my own to read books on the topic, speak with friends and my vet to finally devise my own conditioning strategy to build us up for our first ride. Carefully, I started with "long, slow distance" rides, where I walked, then trotted, then walked again to end the ride.

Next came a change in her feed plan. After consulting with the local feed mill representative, I changed her grain over to a high performance, textured complete feed program. She stayed on the already good quality hay given at the barn, and I added a Vitamin E/selenium supplement to support her muscle cell requirements over long periods of exertion.

Week to week, I lengthened the trot component and slowly reduced the walk sections. Eventually, I added the canter, first only over short distances, then working up to canter/trot sections before a long walk to cool down. We entered our first 25-mile competitive trail ride after 6 months of steady conditioning.

Now at the endurance ride, having made a potentially serious mistake, I wondered what was going to happen to my horse on these strange trails. Alone and walking on the trail, I felt vulnerable and lost. Although I could follow the trail markers, it would be some time before I would get to a vet check. I was also keeping an eye behind me in case another competitor came up from behind me at speed.

I looked up when I heard a rustling ahead of me. To my amazement and wonder, the rider ahead reappeared, coming toward me with Kayla in tow! Both horses were walking calmly, and he courteously asked me if I was injured. When I responded in the negative, he gently handed Kayla's reins to me. Noticing that I was going to get back on, he faced his horse toward us and stood still.

As I mounted, I was in awe that this rider, who was obviously in the race to win, had the generosity and composed frame of mind to stop his rhythm long enough to know that I was safe, on my horse, and able to continue the ride. After a humble "thank you" on my part, he swung his horse around in the tight quarters and sped around the turn, back into his strong canter.

For the remainder of the ride to the first vet stop, Kayla and I matched the horse ahead in speed, with a significant change of strategy from my end – I rated her speed with more insistence at any area that seemed to have questionable footing. We slowed at the 2-mile marker and then walked in calmly and confidently to the 20-mile stop.

In an endurance ride, you can strategize your entry into the hold. Knowing that Kayla usually had a higher pulse and breathing rate than the Arabian horses, it was to my advantage to walk almost to the vet check rather than come in at speed. I had slowed her pace early enough to give her parameters plenty of time to recover, and by the time we stepped into the vet check, she was below the mandatory pulse rate of 64 beats per minute and breathing slower than 12 breaths a minute. The lay vet checked her for possible injuries, palpated her back for any discomfort, listened to her gut sounds, took a look at her capillary refill rate and hydration status. We were sent through with no worries.

I checked my watch – only 2 hours had passed since we had left the start! We had completed the first section at an astounding 10-mile per hour pace – almost twice as fast as our competitive trail rides during the summer! It was then that I realized that the rider ahead was probably one of the most competitive in this ride (he was the eventual winner).

Next came the hold period. During this half-hour mandatory break, we could literally rest. I took her saddle off, got her some pre-made beet pulp mash and grabbed a bite for myself. We both had something to drink and I syringed some electrolytes into Kayla's mouth.

With five minutes left in the hold, I saddled her up again using a clean saddle pad, made sure I had my map on me and mounted. We left on our own at exactly the half-hour mark.

We negotiated the second loop at a more relaxed trot. Somewhere at the 35 mile point after several hours of posting, with my legs cramping and crying out for a break, I started wondering why I was doing this in the first place. For some time, although Kayla kept up a good trot, I caught myself thinking, "And this was my idea of fun?" I realized I was experiencing "the wall" that many long distance riders speak of.

When I could post no longer, I dismounted and walked beside her. For almost half an hour, I worked the tension out of my legs and gave Kayla plenty of time to recover and move without weight on her back. At the final two-mile marker, I remounted and we headed off at a very calm trot, aiming to finish strong. There were just two miles to go, a final vet check and a completion certificate to seal our achievement.

Kayla scored mild hydration loss and slightly lowered gut sounds. However, her pulse, respiration and capillary refill time indicated good recovery parameters. When we went back for the final check a half hour later, her values were back to normal and we were given the all clear – we finished!

As we left the final vet check, I gazed into the infinite wisdom of her deep brown eyes. Kayla's butterfly wink seemed to say, "I knew we could do it." I looked at Kayla with the sort of awe reserved only for the most extraordinary and inspiring moments, thinking, "We really DID that… ?"

Find us at www.HorseListening.com

Keep an eye out for Book 4 in the Horse Listening Collection!

Join us on Facebook and Twitter for daily articles that inspire, educate and share our love for the horse.

ABOUT THE AUTHOR

Kathy Farrokhzad is the author of Horse Listening – The Book and Horse Listening – Book 2. She is also internationally published in national equine magazines and has a monthly column in The Rider. She is also owner and writer of the blog, www.horselsistening.com.

An Equine Canada Competition Coach, she has taught beginner to intermediate students for 20 years. She has worked with all types of horses in a showing, riding, training and teaching capacity in several disciplines.

Kathy practices what she preaches. She embraces the notion that we aren't all superstar riders with superstar horses, riding in the super events with super accolades coming our way. But that doesn't stop us from riding the best we can, putting as much time and effort into riding as possible (within our "real life" constraints and scheduling) and loving our horses. For some of us, striving to be a better rider must become a lifelong aspiration that develops in proportion to our resources. With enough sustained effort, we might even surprise ourselves!

Horse Listening – Book 2: Forward and Round To Training Success

Forward and round is the beginning and the end of all riding. For an inexperienced rider, developing a forward moving horse is the first thing that must be learned in order to achieve even the most basic skills and communication with the horse. For a more educated rider, maintaining a forward and round horse through all the movements is a key factor in keeping the horse happy, healthy and athletic in his work.

"Horse Listening - Book 2: Forward and Round to Training Success" provides practical and theoretical suggestions to improve the training of both the rider and the horse. Compiled from the articles of the popular blog, Horse Listening, this book explains fundamental concepts and skills such as:

- contact
- rider position and aids
- developing suppleness in both horse and rider
- communicating effectively with the horse
- bends, turns and half-halts

Printed in Great Britain
by Amazon

39526093R10119